CANADA

UNITED STATES OF AMERICA

CONFEDERATE STATES OF AMERICA

REPUBLIC OF TEXAS

ROCKY MOUNTAIN STATES

REPUBLIC OF CALIFORNIA

MEXICO

SO-AEX-901

If the SOUTH won GETTYSBURG

Mark Nesbitt

concept by Paul S. Witt

Reliance Publishing Company

RELIANCE

LIBRARY OF CONGRESS CATALOG CARD NO. 80-52561

ISBN 0-937740-01-2

Layout & Design: Colonial Quill Advertising, Arendtsville, PA
Cover photo reference courtesy of NASA

Printed in the United States of America

Reliance Publishing Company
380 Steinwehr Avenue
Gettysburg, PA 17325
(717) 334-1103

To My Mother and Father

Contents

Maps

Introduction

In four years of working for the National Park Service as an historical interpreter at Gettysburg, one question visitors to the park posed stands out in my mind, if not by virtue of frequency asked, then by its impact upon the imagination: "What if the South had won here?"

It is a moot question. History is history—it is past, a progression of events cast in the bronze of time. The best historians can do is piece together the events in the most accurate order existing evidence will allow, and analyze them from there.

I approach this somewhat rhetorical question not as a former historian, but as a writer. Historians, because of the delicate filagree of accuracy and the inherent dubiousness of documentation, are bound to say as little about an event as is needed to avoid inaccuracies; the writer can elaborate on what is known about the event. Historians provide the sketch—writers, the oil paints.

This is no apology to historians for the somewhat radical approach of this book. It needs none. The first half of the work, up to the point where Robert E. Lee changes his battle plan, is an historical piece. Primary sources, such as the *Official Records of the War of the Rebellion* (reports done within weeks after the battle), *The Southern Historical Society Papers* (written after the war by the participants), accounts from *Battles and Leaders* (also postwar) were used whenever the text needed words "from the horses' mouths." If the quotes sometimes do not concur, or seem contradictory, it is because the men who fought the war were human—they had a particular point to make, or a reputation to defend, or, they simply forgot exactly what had happened in the fury of battle years before they sat down to write.

The second half of the book is conjecture. In analyzing the question, "How could the South have won Gettysburg?", I tried to think like a Civil War commander dealing with the knowledge and people available at the time. I leaned heavily on Henri Antoine Jomini's *Summary of the Art of War,* published in 1838. This textbook, it is said, was all but carried into battle by officers, both North and South. I relied only on original maps available to Lee—Jed Hotchkiss' Map, drawn by order of Stonewall Jackson just a few months before the battle, and the 1858 Map of Adams County, from which the Hotchkiss Map was copied. The theories which win the battle for the South come from original post-war accounts of individuals in whose power it was to change the events. Whenever an officer, in his post-war writings, made the statement, "If we had only done this or that, the victory would have been ours," I noted it, and analyzed it in terms of logistics involved, tactics of the day, terrain factors, troop strengths and conditions, time considerations as far as troop movements, and so on. I used no *Deus ex Machina* in rewriting the battle. If I say troops marched to an area and arrived at a certain hour, it is because that is how long it would have taken according to the marching speed of a Civil War unit.

Personalities were hardest to capture. Battles were not (and possibly, are still not) won or lost by numbers of men and the application of text-book tactics, but by the personalities involved. "In war men are nothing," said Napoleon, "but a man is everything." Personalities presented in the first half of the book are authentic—if eyewitnesses said General Lee looked irritated, that is how I have painted him. In the second half of the book, I attempted to keep the personalities congruent with their states of mind in the first half—Ewell still needed more specific orders, Longstreet a little looser rein, to achieve their respective command potentials.

It was an exciting book to do. But I didn't do it all by myself. First, I must thank Paul S. Witt. This is as much his book as it is mine. It was his idea to approach the battle from this standpoint, and he believed in it enough to see it through to its final production. His points of view as a "nonhistorian" (but a highly critical reader) were invaluable in making this not just another dry book on the battle, but something that will spark the imagination of historian and layman alike.

I must also acknowledge the insightful comments of Bob Prosperi, of the National Park Service, as well as Dr. Robert Bloom, Professor of History at Gettysburg College, and John Patterson, Associate Professor of American Studies and History, Pennsylvania State University, Harrisburg Campus. I thank Kathy Carberry for her research assistance, and Mr. George Kackley, Superintendent of Oak Hill Cemetery, Georgetown, and Paula Burns, Washington, D.C. for their help in locating theoretical artillery positions for J. E. B. Stuart's Horse Artillery. I must also mention Donna Trapani for her idea for the cover of the book.

There are also hundreds of others whom I have spoken to, argued with, and received encouragement from during the writing of this book. To them, as well, go special thanks.

Mark Nesbitt
May, 1980

If the SOUTH won
GETTYSBURG

"Now, we are judging men who were laboring to the best that was in them for the things they believed. Our after-knowledge is complete: they could know only a little of the situations then. You sit coldly in your study, removed from the haste and violence and responsibility, and say; there he did wrong; there he erred greatly; there his judgement was unsound. So, of necessity, is history written: to be valuable, it must be critical...."

—John W. Thomason
Jeb Stuart

I. The Seeds of Sectionalism

"There will be no more peace in this land until slavery is done for. I will give them something else to do than to extend slave territory...."

—John Brown,
Abolitionist.

In August of 1618, a Dutch vessel landed at the English colony of Jamestown in Virginia and let off 20 Africans to be used as laborers by the Englishmen who had settled the area eleven years earlier. Over the years more indentured servents—Africans, but more often Irish—were brought to the colonies. Eventually, the Irish indentured servants worked off their debt and were freed. The Black Africans were not.

* * *

In 1793, the Fugitive Slave Law was passed unanimously in the Senate, and by a vast majority in the House. Six new states were shortly thereafter admitted to the Union without question or controversy concerning the fact they were slave-holding states where black men and women were bought and sold as property—like cattle and sheep—legally. Slavery enjoyed tacit acceptance from most Americans. It had become an institution.

* * *

By 1814 however, at the Hartford Convention, concern was expressed over the growing power of slave state representation in Congress versus free state representation, and by 1820, during the legislation over the admission of Missouri, slavery was recognized as having a latitudinal boundary, a political fence across the midsection of America dividing North and South. Not surprisingly, the sectionalism over slavery first drew attention as a political issue rather than a moral one, with politicians more worried about votes than the fate of millions of Black slaves.

* * *

The Missouri Compromise, for the moment in 1821, settled the question of Slave versus Free representation in Congress. But with the rapid expansion of the United States, the balance of power in Congress could not be maintained for long.

* * *

In August of 1831, Nat Turner led a band of fellow-slaves on a rampage through Southampton County, Virginia. His cause was slave revolt; his reason was a vision, a sign from the Lord ordaining him to cast off his bonds and lead his people to freedom. In 48 hours his disciples had killed 57 whites—men, women, and children—indiscriminately.

The reaction is swift and merciless. Blacks, guilty or innocent, are crippled, tortured, decapitated, or burned alive. Even suspicion of involvement in Turner's revolt is cause for execution. Eventually, 3,000 soldiers will crowd Southampton County to quell the disturbance caused by Turner's 70 followers, and in the ensuing months over 100 Blacks are murdered. Though Turner is captured, stands trial, and finally hangs on November 11, 1831, the fear he instilled of slave revolt spread like a disease throughout the South.

The paranoia over slave insurrection and the terror-filled conclusions drawn by whites about the inner-most motives of even the most docile slaves, were handed down to the next generation of Southerners. It was they who had to deal with the ravings in the 1840's and 50's of the growing Abolitionist movement in the North whose one goal was to free the slaves immediately, regardless of the ramifications.

* * *

In 1838, Antoine Henri Jomini, a former member of Napoleon's staff, published a book entitled *Summary of the Art of War*. More than any other

work on the subject, Jomini's careful study of warfare under Napoleon, and his approach to it as an art
rather than a science influenced military minds that
were developing in mid-nineteenth century America.
It was studied at all the major military academies in
the country, both north and south of the Mason-
Dixon line.

Jomini's principles remained integral parts of
the military personalities of men like Thomas J.
Jackson, James Ewell Brown Stuart, Robert E. Lee,
and James Longstreet, as well as their comrades and
adversaries. The blossoming professional warriors of
the 1840's and 50's responded to the spirit of
Napoleon as it was manifested in the writings of
Jomini.

"They want to make war too methodical, too
measured," wrote Jomini. "I would make it brisk,
bold, impetuous, perhaps sometimes even
audacious."

* * *

In 1845 Texas was admitted into the Union as a
slave state. Its acquisition brought on the War with
Mexico, and with the United States' victory came
more land for the Slave Staters and Free Staters to
argue over.

* * *

By the mid-1850's, the Kansas Territory was embroiled in a dispute between Pro-slavery and Anti-
slavery factions. Among the Anti-slavery squatters
was a man named John Brown. On May 24, 1856,
Brown and his sons and three followers staged a raid
in the middle of the night. Calling themselves "The
Northern Army" they stabbed, shot, and axed to
death five Pro-slavery men, in reprisal for the deaths
of several Anti-slavery settlers. Kansas gets the name

"Bleeding Kansas," and the line is drawn—in the new territory you can only be pro or anti slavery, and upon that decision sometimes your life depended.

* * *

The sectional differences between North and South were not confined merely to quarrels over slavery. With the advancing Industrial Revolution and the increase of immigration to the large cities in the North by Europeans, the North became the manufacturing area of the country while the South, with its agrarian way of life, continued to provide the raw materials for the Northern factories. Though the two sections were dependent upon one another, their differences became greater as the middle of the century approached. The typical attitude of the southerner with regards to the rapidly industrializing North was summed up by E. A. Pollard, wartime editor of the "Richmond Examiner." In essence it is a defense of the institution of slavery, but more than that, it is a revealing account of some Southern attitudes:

"...Slavery established in the South a peculiar and noble type of civilization. It was not without attendant vices; but the virtues which followed in its train were numerous.... If the relief of a large class of whites from the demands of physical labour gave occasion in some instances for idle and dissolute lives, yet at the same time it afforded opportunity for extraordinary culture, elevated the standards of scholarship in the South, enlarged and emancipated social intercourse, and established schools of individual refinement. The South had an element in its society—a landed gentry—which the North envied, and for which its substitute was a coarse ostentatious aristocracy that smelt of the trade, and that, however it cleansed itself and aped the elegance of the South, could never entirely subdue a sneaking sense if its inferiority...."

With the South's intellectuals having this kind of attitude and publishing their opinions of "inferior" Northerners in major papers, it is no wonder that sectional differences were reaching the flashpoint.

* * *

In October of 1859, the abolitionist John Brown surfaces again. After months of planning he leads an ardent band of followers to the United States Arensal at Harper's Ferry, Virginia. His objective is to capture the weapons within the arsenal and arm the slaves he expects will flock to join him in the fight for their own freedom.

But the slave insurrection he expects to lead never materializes. Instead, Southerners, reacting violently to the idea of slave revolt, erupt in swift backlash. Locals begin a savage guerilla seige upon Brown and his followers who are trapped within a fire-house along with several hostages. Those of Brown's followers who try to escape are captured, tortured and mutilated. Finally, United States Marines arrive under the command of a Lieutenant-Colonel from staff in Washington named Robert E. Lee. He is accompanied by a young Lieutenant, J. E. B. Stuart who will attempt to talk old John Brown out of his makeshift fortress.

Stuart's parley doesn't work and Brown's followers are attacked by the Marines, who over-run the fire-house and capture Brown and most of his band of Abolitionists. Those not captured were killed in the brief fighting.

Reprisal is quick. In two months Brown is tried, convicted and hanged in Charlestown, Virginia. At the hanging, the scaffold is surrounded by various militia groups, armed and trained, to assure that justice is not thwarted. It seems that all of American history up to 1859 with regards to the growing sectionalism between North and South is symbolized in this man. To the North he represents a new awareness of the problem of slavery. Perhaps more than a little twinge of guilt begins, after Brown's raid, in the hearts of northerners for their acquiesence to the problem of human bondage within their own country.

To the South Brown reveals just how far some Northerners would go to have their institution of slavery abolished.

Commanding the cadets from Virginia Military Institute at the hanging is an awkward, not-too-well-liked professor from the school named Thomas J. Jackson. Soon, he will earn the nickname "Stonewall."

Within the ranks of an elite Richmond militia group guarding the scaffold that Brown hangs from stands a dapper young man with theatrical aspirations. He wishes to be as famous someday as his father and brother, both prominent actors. His name is John Wilkes Booth.

Brown's jailer nervously fingers a note the old man had given him as he left the jail on his way to the scaffold. As Brown's body swings in the cold December wind, the jailer reads again:

"Charlestown, Va, 2 December, 1859. I, John Brown, am now quite *certain* that the crimes of this guilty land: will never be purged away; but with Blood. I had as I now *think vainly* flattered myself that without *very much* bloodshed, it might be done."

* * *

The Election of 1860 was a watershed election. The thing that Southerners feared most was the rise to power of a Republican. Republicanism and Abolition were intertwined in the Southern mind. With splits in the Democratic party dividing the vote, the final tally showed a Republican, Abraham Lincoln from Illinois, to be the winner.

In an attempt to quell fears his election would endanger the South, Lincoln stated in his Inaugural Address on March 4, 1861, that "physically speaking, we cannot separate. We cannot remove our respective sections from each other, nor build an impassable wall between them.... In your hands, my dissatisfied fellow countrymen, and not in mine, is the momentous issue of Civil War. The government will not assail you. You can have no conflict, without being yourselves the aggressors. You have no oath registered in Heaven to destroy the government, while I have the most solemn one to 'preserve, protect, and defend' it...."

His speech was regarded as naive by most Southerners. In light of the fact that by the time he made the speech, seven Southern states had already seceded and the newly formed "Confederacy" had elected and inaugurated its own president nearly a month before, this attitude is understandable.

* * *

In a meeting on April 18, 1861, Francis P. Blair, as representative of Abraham Lincoln, offered to Colonel Robert E. Lee the command of the new United States Army being raised to fight against the forces of the Confederate States. It would seem like a godsend to any professional soldier who had been with the Army for as many long and frustrating years as Lee had. His military life before the impending Civil War had been a relentless adherence to duty— Mexican War, outpost duty, engineering the tedious construction of forts—nothing (with the exception of the few battles in the Mexican War) to give a glimpse of the military artist that lay within him. And now, from Colonel to Commanding General overnight.

Lee politely told the seventy-year-old politician that he "could take no part in an invasion of the Southern states." On April 19, 1861, he resigned his commission from the only profession he had ever known, to cast his lot with his native state and serve in whatever capacity Virginia might need him.

* * *

On April 12, 1861, at 4.30 a.m., artillery batteries in Charleston Harbor, South Carolina, manned by Southerners, opened fire on Fort Sumter, a United States Army fort. After 34 hours of bombardment, Major Richard Anderson surrendered the fort to authorities representing the newly formed Confederate States of America. The rhetoric was over. Armed hostilities in the American Civil War had begun.

Seven states—South Carolina, Mississippi, Florida, Alabama, Georgia, Louisiana, and Texas—have seceeded from the United States. After the bombardment of Fort Sumter, four more pulled out. Although the Confederate battle-flag eventually shows thirteen stars, only eleven ex-United States will comprise the Confederacy, the two extra stars merely representing hopes that two border states, Maryland and Kentucky, will someday join the Confederacy. Maryland did supply troops to both Northern and Southern Armies.

After two minor battles in Virginia and a few small skirmishes out west, the two major armies of the North and South face each other across a small stream less than fifty miles from Washington, D.C. and fight the first major battle of the Civil War. Bull Run (the stream, and the battle as it was called in the North) or First Manassas (the railroad junction after which the battle was named in the South) saw 37,000 Union soldiers defeated and routed by 35,000 Confederates. The North's first "On to Richmond" (the capital of the Confederacy) campaign is stymied and a military legend is born—"There is Jackson standing like a stonewall! Rally behind the Virginians!" Confederate General Barnard Bee dies in the battle shortly after he utters this remark, but the nickname "Stonewall" for Thomas J. Jackson lives on. This was in July of 1861. Northerners and Southerners who believed the war would be over in a few months, begin to realize otherwise.

The Civil War was being fought out west as well. Missouri saw a battle at Wilson's Creek, but the most important strategic area in the Western Theater became the Mississippi River. It was the line of communication and supply to Southern Armies both east and west of it. The North made control of the river one of its main objectives in the war.

At the beginning of April, 1862, the Battle of Shiloh in Tennessee is fought. It was a costly victory for the North, but the country becomes aware of a new personality in the ranks of their officers: U. S. Grant. They call him "Unconditional Surrender" Grant from his demand upon the Confederate forces at Fort Donelson just two months before Shiloh. Lincoln himself begins to refer to the man who is fighting the war the way Lincoln thinks it should be fought. One more hammer blow to the Northern wedge being driven down the Mississippi River is delivered by General John Pope as he forces the fall of the Confederate stronghold on Island No. 10.

But perhaps the most important Northern advance into the Confederacy is taking place in Virginia, on the finger of land that lies between the York and the James Rivers called "The Peninsula." In the largest amphibious landing in history to that date, Union General George McClellan begins to land troops on the Peninsula in March and another "On to Richmond" drive is started.

McClellan moves his army skillfully north along the marshy Peninsula, beating back the Confederates to the very backdoor of Richmond. Northern troops can hear the churchbells ring in Richmond, they are so close. But then, in a series of battles known as the Seven Days' Battles, the Confederate Army under

General Joseph E. Johnston, and later (after Johnston is wounded) Robert E. Lee, attack ferociously, and in a week's time, drive the Union Army back down the Peninsula.

Lee takes over command of the South's largest army, the Army of Northern Virginia. Despite defeats in battles in western Virginia, Lee retains the confidence of President Jefferson Davis enough to warrant his promotion. But the man who was receiving salutations from the populace was a strange figure who won victory after victory in the Shenandoah Valley.

The man they call "Stonewall" has a series of victories unprecedented in the annals of warfare. Marching his troops sometimes thirty or more miles in a day, he gains for them the name of "Jackson's Foot-Cavalry" and whips five separate Union commanders in as many battles in just a month.

Lee and Jackson unite talent and forces to fight the Battle of Second Manassas in August of 1862. Both armies march past the grisly remains of comrades, unearthed from shallow graves by rain, who died in the fighting there a year before. They fight again over once-contested ground, Jackson's men hurling stones at attacking Yankees when they run out of ammunition. Again the Confederates are victorious, and Lee begins to plan an offensive against the North.

Hopes for world-wide recognition of the Confederacy as a new nation and not just a folly, urge the Southern decision to invade the North. Their hopes suffer a setback when their movement northward is stopped near a little tributary to the Potomac called Antietam Creek. The fighting by that creek near the small Maryland town of Sharpsburg will produce more casualties than any other day in American military history.

In December of 1862, Northern troops launch themselves time and again against Confederates entrenched behind a breast high stone wall at Fredericksburg, Virginia. The carnage is incredible, but Union General Burnside wishes to renew the attack the next morning. His officers, realizing the futility of attacking an entrenched position (and some perhaps realizing the dawn of a new type of warfare) talk him out of continuing an attack. The next night he withdraws across the Rappahannock River, and still another drive toward Richmond fails.

While all this continues in America, Great Britain has been debating the issue of diplomatic recognition of the South. In fact, on September 17, 1862, while the Battle of Antietam rages, Britain's Foreign Minister Russel writes to Prime Minister Lord Palmerston that, "The time is come for offering mediation to the United States government, with a view to the recognition of the independence of the Confederates. I agree further that, in case of failure, we ought ourselves to recognize the Southern States as an independent State...." Britain's interest in the matter waned after news of the failure of the first Confederate invasion of the North at Antietam, but victories like Fredericksburg (and more to come) keep the debate of Confederate recognition a hot topic in Parliament.

At the beginning of the new year of 1863, Abraham Lincoln officially issued the Emancipation Proclamation, freeing all slaves in the states fighting against the Union. While in actuality it frees no slaves (and will not until the South is conquered) it does finally make clear the North's political position on slavery. The Proclamation makes the Abolitionists temporarily happy, is of apparently little consequence to the condition of the slave in America, and makes the Union soldier wonder if he is fighting, as he calls it, a "Black Man's War." As the spring of 1863 approaches, Lincoln is slowly becoming the most unpopular president in history. The South hates him, the Northern Democrats despise him, the Radical Republicans are beginning to dislike him because of his lenient policies toward the South, and the growing Peace Party in the North begins to agitate for an end to this already costly war. It was obvious that if it hadn't been for the four-way split of the National Presidential Nominating Convention in 1860, he would probably still be an unknown congressman from Illinois. He signs the draft act establishing quotas for filling the Federal Armies' ranks. Draft riots will ensue. He was accused by the press of making obscene jokes while touring the battlefield of Antietam shortly after the battle. His own cabinet members follow his directions sometimes reluctantly. He refuses to see the Rebellion as a separatist movement, and his only real desire, he states, is to keep the Union intact. With an election coming up in 1864 and rumors of the nomination of the one-time Union Army commander George McClellan (whom Lincoln himself appointed and dismissed twice before) floating in the political wind, it seems unlikely Lincoln will be re-elected.

Neither is his popularity in the North enhanced by his constant shifting of commanders of the Army of the Potomac. "Fighting" Joe Hooker, who gets his nickname from a typographical error (and lends his real name to the large number of women of ill-repute who follow his army everywhere) is assigned command of the Union Army. He finds Robert E. Lee and Stonewall Jackson more than he can handle in a battle at a tiny Virginia hamlet called Chancellorsville. Although Hooker's Army outnumbers the Confederates almost three to one, Jackson rips a page out of Jomini, suggesting to Lee a flank march.

Lee splits his army in the face of the enemy, boldly sending Jackson swinging around the flank and into the rear of Hooker's troops. The victory is nearly complete when Jackson falls, accidentally wounded in the darkness by his own men. He dies a little more than a week later. The Army's grief is deep, the victory at Chancellorsville bittersweet. The South's loss of Jackson is to haunt them.

Though the war is going badly for the North in the Eastern theater, they continue to have good news from the west. Grant, near the middle of May, 1863, begins a seige of Vicksburg, Mississippi, the last Southern stronghold on the great river. Jefferson Davis, who sees his home state threatened and the entire South in deep trouble should Vicksburg fall, tells General Pemberton, his commander there, to hold out at all costs; if Vicksburg falls, the South will be cut in two.

Other Union and Confederate Armies were squaring off, at Charleston, South Carolina, and near Chattanooga, Tennessee. But the main worry for everyone seems to be, what will Lee and his seemingly invincible Army of Northern Virginia do next?

Vicksburg is under pressure, but they can hold out, at least a little while longer. The Southern Army under Lee's command has been rolling up victories. Great Britain is still holding out on recognition of the Confederacy. Morale in the Southern ranks has never been higher. The poor farmers in Virginia have suffered for two years trying not only to support themselves and the Southern Army's needs, but also the wants of the Northern Army which commandeers everything for their hungry troops while Northern farmers have abundant, untouched supplies. The time is ripe. Lee and Davis decide: invade the North. On June 3, 1863, Lee begins his march toward the Shenandoah Valley, then turns his army's tanned faces and burnished weapons toward the North and fate.

II. Invasion

June 3, 1863

"An invasion of the enemy's country breaks up all his preconceived plans, and relieves our country of his presence, and we subsist while there on his resources...."

—R. E. Lee

Throughout the month of June, the Confederate Army of Northern Virginia lumbers northward. Ewell's Corps is in the lead. Longstreet's men follow. A. P. Hill's Corps stays at Fredericksburg to watch the Union Army for a while, then they, too, follow. They move into the Shenandoah Valley, the Blue Ridge Mountains forming a natural barrier from nosey Yankee cavalry patrols, since the gaps in the mountains can be easily plugged by a handful of Confederates.

This is only the second invasion of the North— Southern politicians would have them wage a totally defensive war if they had their way—the first invasion having been turned back at the Battle of Antietam nine months before. Now, with British recognition of the Confederacy looming north of the Mason-Dixon line (provided they can win a victory there), morale in the Confederate Army is at a peak. Seventy-five thousand strong, flushed with the victories at Fredericksburg and Chancellorsville, the Confederates turn northward, marching, they are certain, to victory and the end of the war.

Their advance along the Valley Turnpike is easy, except for the growing heat of summer. Ewell's men drive Milroy's Union troops out of Winchester, Virginia, on the 14th and 15th of June, clearing the Valley for the Confederate advance. Sharp cavalry battles are fought at Aldie, Middleburg, and Upperville, Virginia, about the same time. Lee's cavalry commander, J. E. B. ("Jeb") Stuart holds the prying Yankees at bay.

On June 16th, Confederate forces move across the Potomac River. With Rebels now on Northern soil, Pennsylvania panics. Harrisburg, the capital of the state, becomes the scene of frenzied anxiety. Wagons loaded with goods from southern Pennsylvania cross the Susquehanna River, as farmers and merchants try to escape with as much private property as they can. The North feels, for the second time in nine months, the icy fear of war on their own doorsteps.

* * *

June 22, 1863

[To] Lieut. Gen. R. S. Ewell:
...I am much gratified at the success which has attended your movements, and feel assured, if they are conducted with the same energy and circumspection, it will continue. Your progress and direction will, of course, depend upon the development of circumstances. If Harrisburg comes within your means, capture it....

—R. E. Lee

If the South Won Gettysburg

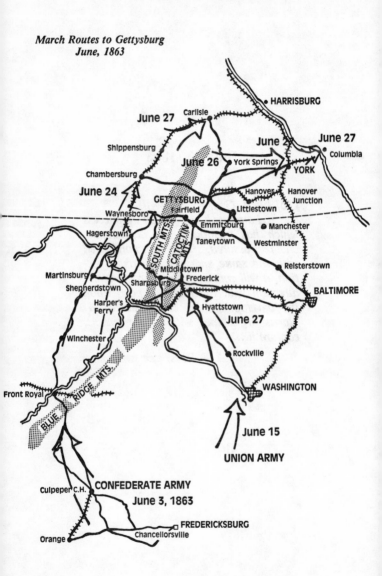

March Routes to Gettysburg
June, 1863

HARRISBURG

June 27 Carlisle

June 2

June 27

Shippensburg Columbia

June 26 York Springs

Chambersburg YORK

June 24 Hanover Hanover Junction

GETTYSBURG

Waynesboro Fairfield Littlestown

Hagerstown Emmitsburg Manchester

Taneytown Westminster

Martinsburg Middletown

Shepherdstown Sharpsburg Frederick Reisterstown

Harper's Ferry Hyattstown BALTIMORE

Winchester June 27

Rockville

Front Royal WASHINGTON

June 15

UNION ARMY

Culpeper C.H. CONFEDERATE ARMY

June 3, 1863 FREDERICKSBURG

Orange Chancellorsville

SOUTH MTS CATOCTIN MTS BLUE RIDGE MTS.

What of the troops facing the invading Confederates? The Army of the Potomac, the North's largest army in the field, is over 97,000 strong in the summer of 1863. Its ranks have been bolstered up by the addition of troops from the static defenses of Washington. Its theater of operations always includes Washington, D.C., the capital of the North, whose protection dictates the Army's every move. As the Confederate Army swings wide to the west of Washington, the Union Army takes the inside track, constantly trying to stay between the Confederates and the capital.

There are also various Northern units (some made up of militia outfits who had never heard the whine of a hostile minie ball before) assigned to protect the strategic points in the North—Harrisburg, Pittsburgh, Baltimore, New York. The communications between the units and Washington are also of interest.

From Darius Couch, commanding what troops there are in the military Department of the Susquehanna near Harrisburg, to Edwin Stanton, Secretary of War in Washington: "Sir:... In case the rebels advance in large force, I believe from my present knowledge of the Susquehanna that we can prevent them crossing.... You will readily understand what kind of force I have, when a few regiments, with a sprinkling of nine-month's men in them, are the veterans. The New York troops look very well, but are without much confidence in themselves. My little artillery is all raw; my cavalry the same...."

Couch is optimistic to a fault when he says he thinks he can prevent the Confederates from crossing the shallow Susquehanna. The nine-month's men he refers to have signed up to serve only that length of time, barely enough to train them. And a lack of confidence in the troops from New York means that they probably have never seen a battle; Couch himself can feel their apprehension about having to defend the capital of Pennsylvania against Lee's veterans. "If" Harrisburg comes within Ewell's means, as Lee's order states, he should have no trouble capturing it.

* * *

June 23, 1863

Lee's orders to his cavalry commander were unclear, and with a man as full of initiative as Jeb Stuart, if you only wanted him to go so far, you had to tell him. Tactically, the ideal thing a cavalry leader can do on an invasion is to divert the enemy's attention from the main force while still supplying his main force with information about the enemy. But how to do this?

As the Confederate main columns swing northward, the Blue Ridge Mountains on their east, Jeb Stuart has a plan: sweep around the enemy's rear, pass between the Union Army and their capital Washington, cut communications and supply lines between the two and throw confusion into both the army and the politicians as to just where Lee's army really is, then cross the Potomac and rejoin the Confederate Army somewhere north of it.

Lee thinks about Stuart's plan and talks to Longstreet about it. Longstreet recognizes what Stuart is trying to do—that a ride around the Union Army will divert their attention from the Confederate main force more than simply plugging up the gaps in the Blue Ridge Mountains. Longstreet thinks it will work.

Lee replies to Stuart on June 22, 1863: "If you find that he (the Union Army) is moving northward, and that two brigades can guard the Blue Ridge and take care of your rear, you can move with the other three into Maryland and take position on General Ewell's right." He tells Stuart that Ewell is on his way to the Susquehanna River via Chambersburg and Emmitsburg. Lee sends a message later in the day to Ewell that Stuart will cross the Potomac with three brigades and report to him in Pennsylvania to cover his right. Longstreet sees the letter to Stuart and approves, and adds that Stuart should move into Pennsylvania by his proposed route in the rear of the enemy, something that Lee did not include in that communique.

Another order dated the 23rd comes from Lee: "If General Hooker's Army remains inactive you can leave two brigades to watch him and withdraw the three others, but should he not appear to be moving northward, I think you had better withdraw this side of the mountains tomorrow night, cross at Shepherdstown next day, and move over to Fredericktown." The next sentence is important—"You will, however, be able to judge whether you can pass around their army without hindrance, doing them all the damage you can, and cross the river east of the mountains." He tells Stuart after that to move and connect with Ewell's right flank across the Potomac. Still, in the orders, he leaves it to the discretion of Stuart whether he will take the route around the rear of the Union Army or not.

That night, when Lee's orders reached Stuart's camp, it was pouring rain. Major McClellan, Stuart's adjutant, walks from the porch of a nearby house where he was allowed to stay out of the rain to handle messages, to Stuart who was sleeping, as was his habit, in the rain and mud with his troopers, and woke the General. McClellan read him the orders by the light of a lantern. Jeb Stuart says nothing, but makes his decision alone, in the pouring rain of that night, to sweep around the rear of the enemy.

* * *

June 25, 1863

As the Rebel Army makes its way deeper into Pennsylvania, the major cities of the North are in near panic. Harrisburg is filling up with farmers and tradesmen from the more southern counties, all fleeing with as much livestock and goods as their wagons can carry. Once across the Susquehanna River, they feel they will be safe. The city of Baltimore is ordered to send every Union soldier who arrives there immediately to Washington. The Capital itself is stripped of troops down to the minimum to supply the Army of the Potomac. These three cities—Harrisburg, Baltimore, and Washington—engage in a dispute between themselves over which needs troops more.

Washington, of course, gets the preference when troops are available. The problem is that most of the troops in Washington are given to the army in the field because, they reason, it is better to fight a battle and attempt to stop the Confederates somewhere north of Washington, than to fall back within the city and fight there. So, as the near panicky correspondence to General Heintzleman (who commands the Department of Washington) indicates, military manpower around the big cities in the North grows dangerously low as the month of June wears on into the beginning of July.

Heintzleman's job is not made any easier by correspondence such as the letter he receives on June 25, 1863 from Brigadier General J. G. Barnard at the headquarters of the Chief Engineer of the Defenses of Washington. Though a large number of earthen forts were constructed at the beginning of the war, and more were in the plans, all of a sudden Barnard complains that "it was never supposed that the forts alone would protect Washington. Aided by darkness or fog, bodies of cavalry may pass between them, or columns of infantry may if [aided] by artillery and infantry attacks upon the works themselves, the latter being fully employed otherwise, contrive to pass through...."

Poor Heintzelman was probably wondering why they ever bothered to build the forts to begin with if they are of no use in defending the city. The bad news from Barnard continues:

"...Nay, further, the works themselves are not deemed secure without full garrisons—i.e., the requisite infantry supports to man the parapets.

"I understand that not only are there no troops left to man the riflepits and to support the artillerymen of the forts, but that even the number of artillerymen is not up to standard."

Barnard goes on to say that the safety of Washington is dependent upon Hooker's Army of the Potomac, and its ability to keep itself between the Confederate Army sweeping north of the capital, and the city of Washington itself. One other thing bothered Barnard: the wooden bridges of the city and their vulnerability to fire—but not fires set by the Confederate Army.

"...In case of attack there are enough secessionists in the city who would, if they could secretly, burn these structures, knowing their immense importance to the defense...."

* * *

Lee senses, with that old soldier's sense, that those people with whom the safety of the Northern capital is entrusted, are feeling a bit insecure about having the Confederate Army on the loose in the North. He writes to Jefferson Davis, "You will see that apprehension for the safety of Washington and their own territory has aroused the Federal Government and people to great exertions, and it is incumbent upon us to call forth all our energies...."

He also informs Davis of the fact that he will

have to abandon communications with the capital at Richmond. It takes troops to guard the telegraph wires and stations along the invasion route, and Lee feels he needs every man. He ends the communication with the hope that things in Vicksburg will end up well for the Confederacy, probably knowing that the outcome in Mississippi is, in many aspects, dependent upon his own success.

Again, in Northern correspondence between General Schenck, who is charged with protecting Baltimore from the Confederates, and General-in-Chief Henry Halleck in Washington, the anxiousness can be cut with a knife:

"Major-General Schenck,
        Baltimore, Md.:   (4 p.m.)
    It is important that all troops that have arrived or may arrive at Baltimore from New York, after the receipt of my order, be forwarded here. They are greatly needed.
                H. W. Halleck,
                General-in-Chief"

"Major General Halleck,
        Washington, D.C.:   (5:30 p.m.)
    The Fifty-fifth Regiment New York State Militia, 175 strong, has just arrived. Do you include this in your order to forward to Washington all New York regiments that may hereafter arrive?
                Robt. C. Schenck"

"Major General Schenck,
        Baltimore, Md.:   (9:50 p.m.)
    My order to send troops to Washington means precisely what it says. I cannot make it more definite.
                H. W. Halleck,
                General-in-Chief"

June 26, 1863

A new name begins to pop up in the correspondence; the name of a small town not far from the Maryland border in Pennsylvania—Gettysburg.

There is nothing notable about the town in June of 1863. Mostly agricultural, its only claim to fame and posterity was that the Congressman Thaddeus Stevens once had a law office on Chambersburg Street. It had all the little virtues and vices any rural town of 2400 inhabitants in Victorian America would have, except for the fact that it was a bit close to the border of a state that was "riding the fence" as to which course it would take. Some of the Southern sympathies from Maryland crept into Gettysburgians daily lives.

* * *

General Couch in Harrisburg receives correspondence from a Major Haller of the 7th U.S. Infantry:

"Threw Colonel Jennings' regiment 3 miles in advance of Gettysburg this morning in a good position. The rebel advance guard approaching caused him to fall back...."

And, later that evening:

"Major Knox and Captain Bell have arrived. Rebels in Gettysburg. Ran our cavalry through town; fired on them; no casualties. Horses worn out. Ordered all troops to York, to rendezvous at Camp Franklin...."

* * *

Confederates move through the town of Gettysburg on the 26th, on their way toward the Susquehanna. Looking at a map of the town, it would seem inevitable that an army marching through this part of Pennsylvania would pass through Gettysburg—eleven roads all come together within a block of the center of town.

* * *

Back in Washington, General Heintzelman, in the best of bureaucratic traditions, passes General Barnard's correspondence concerning the shabby state of the defenses of Washington to his superior, Halleck. "Old Brains", as many of his contemporaries called him ("Old Woodenhead" as many others called him) was more of a soldier by the book than inventive or creative. Lincoln regarded him as "little more than a first rate clerk." He had a nervous habit of rubbing his elbows, and the more important the problem, the more tactless he became. He, no doubt, nearly wore out his uniform sleeves upon receiving Barnard's message and the additional comments by Heintzelman:

"When the 10,000 men were sent to General Dix, nearly emptying the rifle-pits, General Hooker's army held the line of the Rappahannock. Since General Hooker has fallen back to the front of the Defenses [of Washington], he has obtained from this department about 6,000 cavalry; from General Abercrombie over 8,000 men; General Crawford's command, 4,967 men; and Colonel Jewett, from Poolesville, 2,282 men; making 15,249, or, including the cavalry and the force sent to General Dix, there have been lost to the Defenses at least 30,000 veteran soldiers.

"To replace them, we have the employees of the Quartermaster's and Commissary Departments organized, but they cannot be made at all effective or available unless they are called out once or twice a week until they get some idea of their duties....

"I deem it very important to have the citizens formed into some organization, such as home

45

guards, to aid in the defense in case of an attack. It is very desirable to do so in such a manner as not to add to the unnecessary alarm that already exists.

"My communication of yesterday will have informed the general of the condition of the garrisons, and the entire want of infantry to line the parapets and rifle-pits."

* * *

Troops. Where will they come from? Washington has been stripped of at least 30,000 men; enough to persuade the commander of the Department of Washington to suggest attempting the organization of the civilian populace into armed units. This would be a difficult undertaking since it takes time for men to learn to drill, to operate the type of artillery that was placed in the forts, to act as soldiers when under fire. Guaranteed, they would not be enthusiastic about serving, or they would have joined the army already. And if General Barnard's estimation of the number of southern sympathizers was accurate, what kind of soldier would the average citizen of Washington have made?

But an even greater problem existed: most of the forts around Washington faced south, toward Virginia. No one would expect a Southern attack from the north....

* * *

June 27, 1863

"Direct that the cavalry be sent to the advance of Frederick, in the direction of Gettysburg and Emmitsburg, and see what they can of the movements of the enemy."

Joseph Hooker,
Major-General

Another telegraph reaches Stanton at the War Department at 5:15 p.m. on the evening of the 27th. It is from Major General Wool in charge of troops in New York City. It is interesting not so much in that it shows compliance with Halleck's order of the 25th to send every available soldier to Washington, but in the intimation of Wool's last sentence:

"I am sending to Washington every man able to do service. They are also sending all the militia of the city to Pennsylvania....Major General Halleck has called for the company stationed at Sandy Hook, in the fort under construction, to man the guns already mounted. They cannot be spared. To send them away...will cause great excitement among friends as well as foes, and you have too many of the latter in this city."

* * *

From Chambersburg in Pennsylvania, General Lee issues the following order to his invading troops. It is a testimony not only to the character of the Confederate Commanding General, but also to the character of the American Civil War. It is also the death-knell of this type of warfare. Because of men like Lee and the troops he commanded (and fought against) a latter-day British diplomat and student of the American Civil War, Winston Churchill, would call it "the last war among gentlemen."

"General Orders,Hdqrs. Army of Northern Virginia,
    No. 73.   Chambersburg, Pa., June 27, 1863.

The commanding general has observed with marked satisfaction the conduct of the troops on the march, and confidently anticipates results commensurate with the high spirit they have manifested.

No troops could have displayed greater fortitude, or better performed their arduous marches of the past ten days...

There have, however, been instances of forgetfulness on the part of some that they have in keeping the yet unsullied reputation of this army...

The commanding general considers no greater disgrace could befall the army, and through it, our whole people, than the perpetration of barbarous outrages upon the unarmed and defenseless, and the wanton destruction of private property, that have marked the course of the enemy in our own country...

It must be remembered that we make war only upon armed men, and that we can not take vengeance for the wrongs our people have suffered without lowering ourselves in the eyes of all whose abhorrence has been excited by the atrocities of our enemies...

The commanding general, therefore, earnestly exhorts the troops to abstain, with most scrupulous care, from unnecessary or wanton injury to private property, and he enjoins upon all officers to arrest and bring to summary punishment all who shall in any way offend against orders on this subject.

> R. E. Lee,
> General"

A resident of Chambersburg, writing of his experiences as a civilian while the invading hordes marched through his town said, "Candor compels me to say that in the main these humane regulations were observed."

* * *

June 28, 1863

"How much depends in military matters on one master mind!!"
—A. Lincoln

Voices and commotion outside his tent awaken Major General George Gordon Meade. It was three in the morning. His Fifth Corps of the Union Army had marched to Frederick, Maryland and was encamped there. The tent flap opens and Colonel James Hardie from the staff of General-in-Chief Halleck enters.

He tells General Meade jokingly that he comes as the bearer of trouble. Meade, still half asleep, is not amused; rather, he takes Hardie seriously and begins to defend his actions of the past few weeks against the anticipated news that he has been dismissed from command or arrested. Hardie hands him the communique from the adjutant general's office, and Meade discovers suddenly that he had been made commander of the Army of the Potomac.

His military abilities were summed up by Lee upon hearing of his appointment: "General Meade will commit no blunder in my front, and if I make one he will make haste to take advantage of it." Though ungainly in appearance, he is thorough and meticulous, and nearly always in control when it comes to the welfare of his troops in battle. He possesses, however, an explosive temper when confronted by negligence or laziness in subordinates. He is told upon taking command of the army to "maneuver and fight in such a manner as to cover the capital and Baltimore....Should General Lee move upon either...it is expected that you will either anticipate him or arrive with him to give him battle."

* * *

J. E. B. Stuart is in Maryland, having crossed the Potomac at Rowser's Ford. Upon entering Rockville about noon, his men discover they have struck the Union supply line from Washington to the Army of the Potomac west of the city. Rolling towards them was a supply train of over 125 wagons, filled to the brim with oats, corn, hams, hard-tack, bacon, and whiskey. To the tired and famished cavalrymen, the booty was irresistable.

Good fortune, without a doubt. Brand new wagons, fresh mules, and provisions for men and horses! The decision was made or assumed that they would all have to be brought back to General Lee and the Army.

* * *

The man called Harrison was a spy for the Confederate Army. We don't know his first name, or even if Harrison was his real last name. But if Harrison was enigmatic, he was also incredibly efficient.

Meade discovered that he had been made commander of the Army of the Potomac around 3:00 a.m. on June 28, 1863. Before the day was out, Robert E. Lee knew it too. The carrier of this information was Harrison, who also told him that the Union Army was now north of the Potomac and in hot pursuit of Lee—the first information concerning his enemy's location that Lee had. The spy also told him the approximate Yankee strength and relative dispositions. To Lee, who was starved for information concerning his enemy, Harrison was a godsend, even if he was a member of a fraternity of doubtful fidelity.

Harrison was doing the duty, many would say later, that Stuart should have been doing. Where was the cavalry on the invasion north? Why wasn't Stuart ahead of the Confederate Army, or scouting around its flanks to ascertain where the enemy was relative to the Confederate force? Lee himself pondered where his reknowned Stuart was.

He should have known though, and Longstreet too, for that matter, that Stuart was swinging in a broad arc around the rear of the Union Army, between their enemy and his capital of Washington. It was Lee who gave Stuart those discretionary orders on the 23rd of June: "You will, however, be able to judge whether you can pass around their army without hindrance, doing them all the damage you can, and cross the river east of the mountains." And Longstreet endorsed the idea.

If Lee and Longstreet could have read a dispatch sent at 4:05 p.m. on the 28th from M. C. Meigs, the Quartermaster General of the Union Army in Washington, to General Ingalls, Meade's Chief Quartermaster with the Army of the Potomac, they both could have seen that Stuart was indeed doing his job in the rear of the Northern Army. The language is acerbic as Meigs relates Fitzhugh Lee's capturing of the wagon train near Rockville:

"The bootees and socks will be ordered, and will be sent as soon as a safe route and escort can be found. Last fall I gave orders to prevent the sending of wagon trains from this place to Frederick without escort. The situation repeats itself, and gross carelessness and inattention to military rule this morning cost us 150 wagons and 900 mules, captured by cavalry between this and Rockville....

All the cavalry of the Defenses of Washington was swept off by the army [of the Potomac], and we are now insulted by burning wagons 3 miles outside of Tennallytown.

Your communications are now in the hands of General Fitzhugh Lee's [Confederate Cavalry] brigade.

M. C. Meigs
Quartermaster-General"

And if Lee thought his information from his cavalry was scarce, the situation couldn't have been much better in the Union high command. Cutting through red tape, Lincoln sends this message to General Couch in Harrisburg concerning rumors he has heard:

"Major-General Couch:
    What news now? What are the enemy firing at 4 miles from your works?
                                        A. Lincoln."

Couch replies the enemy has not yet made any show of attacking in force, but are burning railroad bridges. He estimates that there are approximately 15,000 of the enemy in the vicinity of Harrisburg, and again in a dispatch the name of a small Pennsylvania town pops up: Gettysburg.

On the morning of June 29th, J.E.B. Stuart picks up a local newspaper in Maryland and discovers that Ewell is heading toward Harrisburg per Lee's orders. About 5:00 p.m., his cavalry gets in a sharp fight with a detachment of Blue cavalry at Westminster, Maryland. He whips the Yankees, then moves north of the town for the night's bivouac. He has made only about 50 miles in two days—not good for cavalry on a campaign. He could make twice that much if he tried. But that would necessitate the burning of the wagon train he captured. A commander must weigh many things in his decisions—what would be the effect upon morale if he ordered the burning of supplies and wagons that his men knew the army needed; what would General Lee say if he knew that Stuart had sent much needed supplies and wagons up in smoke? Stuart ponders the questions, and decides to keep the wagons with him. He will catch up with Lee a little later than planned. Besides, Stuart knows that he left Lee with more cavalry than he took away. He knows that General Lee does not lack cavalry escort, and so proceeds toward his ordered rendezvous with General Ewell in Pennsylvania.

* * *

June 30, 1863

"Major General Halleck:
    Lee is falling back suddenly from the vicinity of Harrisburg, and concentration appears to be at or near Chambersburg. The object apparently a sudden move against Meade....

                H. Haupt
            Brigadier-General"

Brigadier General Pettigrew had been to Gettysburg in the afternoon looking for shoes for his men. Many of his ragged Confederates were barefoot, which was fine for the red-clay roads of Virginia, but these cursed Yankee roads of Pennsylvania with their rocks and outcroppings would tear a soldier's feet to ribbons.

He never made it into the town itself though, and so was unsuccessful in his quest. He had run into some Union cavalry pickets—just a few of them— but enough to deduce that they were probably backed up by infantry somewhere behind the ridges just west of the town. Besides, General Early had been through the town days before, and if there had been any shoes in Gettysburg, Early's men would have them on their feet at this very moment. Prudently, Pettigrew had come back to Cashtown and told his story to General Heth, his commander.

General Hill, the corps commander, was there now, and Heth has Pettigrew tell the details to the red-headed general.

Hill says that his information about the disposition of the Yankee infantry was different. Their main body was supposed to be back aways, still in Maryland. He was certain that what Pettigrew saw was merely a scouting detachment.

"If there is no objection," Heth broke in, "I will take my division tomorrow to Gettysburg and get those shoes."

Pettigrew stood silent as fate swirled around him, and heard Hill say the four words that would bring on the Battle of Gettysburg:

"None in the world."

* * *

The concern about the Defenses of Washington is making its way upward through the bureaucratic system in Washington. Secretary of War Stanton sends a message to the General-in-Chief Halleck with his own suggestions as to how the city should and must be protected.

"Old Brains" needs the advice of a civilian like he needs another enemy among the politicos of Washington. His terse answer to Stanton does nothing to endear him to the Secretary of War, who already is forming the opinion (which he eventually verbalizes) that Halleck is the "greatest scoundrel and most bare-faced villain in America." Categorically, Halleck points out each reason why Stanton's idea of planting batteries at the avenues of approach to the city is not feasible from a military man's viewpoint. He says to leave things in the hands of the engineers.

Affairs in Washington are beginning to grow tense.

* * *

III. The Battle Of Mistakes

July 1, 1863

"Battles have been stated by some writers to be the chief and deciding features of war. This assertation is not strictly true."

—Jomini

Concentration

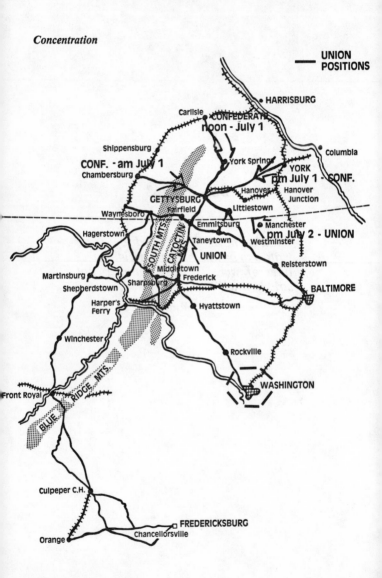

It is about 8:00 a.m., Wednesday, the First of July. Heth's men advance toward the little town of Gettysburg from the west in battle-line—spread out, shoulder-to-shoulder, their line straddling the Chambersburg Pike. They had brushed aside some Union cavalry pickets earlier, and now, as they looked up the ridge into the sun from the little stream they were crossing, they saw more Yankees.

Pop! A carbine goes off. Pop! Another. Pop! Pop! Now a crackle of fire along the ridge. Heth's men return the fire and continue to advance. Another cavalry patrol, they think. This will not take long.

But it does. The Union cavalrymen are using their Sharps carbines. They load from the rear, unlike the infantry weapons which load from the front, and while they do not have the range or the power of a muzzle-loader, a man can load while lying down, making him a very small target. They are quick to load as well, and so, even though outnumbered, General Buford's Union cavalrymen hold the Confederates at bay, since they are firing three and four times as fast.

As soon as the firing starts, couriers race out from the rear of both lines with urgent requests: Bring reinforcements, on the double-quick!

Ten a.m. The Union infantry arrives from several miles south of the town of Gettysburg. They relieve the worn-out cavalry. It is incredible how tired a man can get in battle—two hours seem like forever —physical and mental exhaustion. More Confederates flock to the area as well, and renew their attacks.

Major-General John F. Reynolds, commander of the Union infantry coming up, turns in the saddle to shout an order to his men behind—he led his men rather than followed them into battle—and is struck in the head by a minie ball. He had been offered the command of the Army of the Potomac before

Meade, but turned it down. The decision cost him his life.

The fighting lasts until around noon, then dies down. But by now troops from both sides are rushing toward Gettysburg. Union forces spread out north of the town, roughly extending their existing lines to the west of it. About 2:30 p.m. the fighting breaks out again. Confederates who had been in Carlisle, 30 miles north of Gettysburg, have arrived upon the field near Oak Hill, and finding Yankees before them, attack furiously.

The Southerners are on Oak Hill and firing their cannon down at the Union soldiers in the open fields before them. The terrain is almost perfect for artillery. Although the Confederates probably didn't know it then, the troops they faced were Howard's Eleventh Corps, the very same outfit that "Stonewall" Jackson had so completely surprised and humiliated at Chancellorsville. They were holding pretty well so far though. But then, suddenly, it seemed like Chancellorsville all over again.

From the east come Jubal Early's men, backed up by plenty of artillery firing from that direction. Without orders, unexpectedly, the entire Confederate line surges forward—from the Fairfield Road to the Heidlersburg Road—in a giant, bristling semi-circle. It is 4:00 p.m.

The Union line collapses before the onslaught. They begin an orderly retreat, but once in the town, their lines broken by the streets and houses, the retreat turns into a rout. There are a few pockets of stiff Yankee resistance, but for the most part, Confederates follow them through the town, sometimes only a block away, sometimes even closer than that. They capture Yankees by the hundreds.

Once through the town, the Union soldiers see the high ground south of it, and with the primordial instinct of all soldiers, past, present, and probably future, they go for it. There is a cemetery on the hill, and a sign at the gate: "Anyone found using firearms in the Cemetery will be prosecuted."

The general officers finally choose this hill and the ridges that extend from it as their position to defend. As reinforcements come up from Maryland, they will be placed accordingly. But for now, reinforcements are still miles and hours away.

And so, Union soldiers trickle back through the town, to the high ground south of it. Whipped, exhausted, they had just been beaten again by Bobby Lee and his ragged devils—and they knew it. They had just run, most of the time as fast as they could go, close to two miles, to get here. All of this after fighting several hours. The temperature most of the day had been in the high 70's, and along the hill could be heard the sounds of men trying to find their units, reorganize, but most of all, rest: "Where's water?" "82nd Illinois?" "I've got to rest. Can't go one step more."

* * *

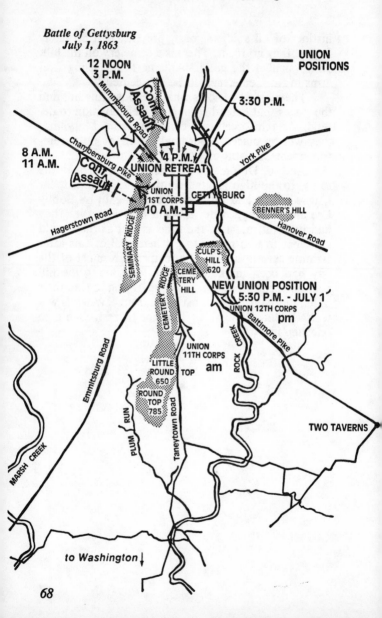

Battle of Gettysburg July 1, 1863

UNION POSITIONS

12 NOON
3 P.M.

Mummasburg Road

Conf. Assault

3:30 P.M.

8 A.M.
11 A.M.

Chambersburg Pike

Conf. Assault

4 P.M.
UNION RETREAT

York Pike

UNION 1ST CORPS
10 A.M.

GETTYSBURG

BENNER'S HILL

Hagerstown Road

Hanover Road

SEMINARY RIDGE

CULP'S HILL 620

CEMETERY HILL

NEW UNION POSITION 5:30 P.M. - JULY 1

CEMETERY RIDGE

UNION 12TH CORPS
pm

Emmitsburg Road

UNION 11TH CORPS
am

LITTLE ROUND TOP 650

ROUND TOP 785

PLUM RUN

ROCK CREEK

Baltimore Pike

Taneytown Road

TWO TAVERNS

MARSH CREEK

to Washington ↓

68

If the South Won Gettysburg

It is 5:00 p.m. General James Longstreet rides up the gentle west slope of Seminary Ridge, past wounded and stragglers, past Lee's staff urging privates of the guard to hurry with the headquarters tents so they can get on with the paperwork of the battle, past the stone house on the north side of the road, and up to his commander at the crest of the ridge. Longstreet, commander of the Army's First Corps, is Lee's senior subordinate. The affection between them is unusual: Lee calls Longstreet "my old war horse"; Longstreet's incessant opinions on strategies and tactics border on insubordination, but Lee, time after time, forgives him. He is forty-two years old, physically strong and active, handsome, tall, well-proportioned. He is not the gambler in battle that the audacious Jackson was, and so shares none of the reputation of "Stonewall." But, as he exchanges the usual pleasantries of military protocol with Lee on the crest of Seminary Ridge, he is respected by all for his handling of troops in battle.

Five minutes pass; ten, while Longstreet studies the Union position through his field glasses. He finally turns to Lee:

"If we could have chosen a point to meet our plans of operation, I do not think we could have found a better one than that upon which they are concentrating. All we have to do is throw our army around by their left, and we shall interpose between the Federal Army and Washington. We can get a strong position and wait, and if they fail to attack us we shall have everything in condition to move back to-morrow night in the direction of Washington selecting beforehand a good position into which we can place our troops to receive battle next day. Finding our object is Washington or that army, the Federals will be sure to attack us. When they attack, we shall beat them, as we proposed to do before we left Fredericksburg, and the probabilities are that the fruits of our success will be great.''

Lee watched as Longstreet made broad, sweeping gestures with his field glasses. Lee wondered, did he mean a tactical or strategic movement? What effect would it have upon the men to abandon ground immediately after they had fought so hard to gain it? What was the topography like south of this town? What were the Union troop strengths in Washington which would be in the Confederate rear if Lee took Longstreet's advice? No. Without Stuart's cavalry here, not enough is known about the terrain and the enemy's position to be able to insure a successful march across the face of the Union Army.

"General Longstreet, if the enemy is there tomorrow, we must attack him."

* * *

In the eyes of Confederate General Isaac Trimble, it was a simple enough thing from here: the Union soldiers—what was left of them—clung desperately to the side of the hill before them, with little artillery support, no reinforcements within several miles, defeated, demoralized, whipped once again. Therefore, Trimble knows, we must attack, and soon. Press the Yankees and they will crumble, and run like the devil back along the roads they came up until they crash headlong into their own reinforcements. Then they, in all probability, will run too. A simple thing to win the battle within the next few hours.

In fact, General Lee had predicted this situation at their last meeting, when Trimble rejoined the army a few weeks ago, after recovering from the wound he received at Second Manassas. Trimble thought he could remember Lee's words almost verbatim: "I shall throw an overwhelming force on their advance, crush it, follow up the success, drive one corps back on another, and by successive repulses and surprise before they can concentrate create a panic and virtually destroy the army." And here it is; the very opportunity Lee had foreseen.

Trimble sees Ewell with his staff near a house on the edge of town and rides up to him.

"Well, General," says Trimble, barely able to hide his elation at the situation, "we have had a grand success; are you not going to follow it up and push our advantage?"

"General Lee has instructed me not to bring on a general engagement without orders," replies Ewell in his warbling, bird-like voice, "and I will wait for them."

There was something different about the once hard-riding, profane, quick-tempered Ewell that almost everyone had noticed. He is not the same fierce warrior of 1861-62 who had, single-handedly, cursed out a raiding band of Yankees in the middle of the night clad only in his nightshirt. Many date his change in personality from the battle at Groveton, where he loses a leg and acquires the nurse who cares for him as his wife. He rides to battle now in a carriage, and swears no more, having been transformed into a devout Christian by his wife. He is fidgety and nervous, and more and more, it seems to those around him, in need of the support of other officers before acting upon military matters. Perhaps this occurs to Trimble as he points out to Ewell that a general engagement had just been fought, that Lee's orders certainly could not apply now, and that the time to press the advantage they had won, was now.

Ewell seems disturbed at Trimble's remarks, but says nothing. Trimble presses the point, but again Ewell says that he could not act without orders.

Trimble mounts his horse and rides off to see for himself the terrain which the Yankees occupy.

The damn fool!, thinks Trimble. Did Ewell lose his military judgement with his leg? A corporal could see the advantage of moving against the Yankees at this moment. There, that hill right there. The wooded hill next to the one with the cemetery on it where the Yankees are forming. It commands the enemy—or us—depending upon who seizes it first. He turns and rides back to Ewell.

"General, *there*," says Trimble, pointing to Culp's Hill, "is an eminence of commanding position, and not now occupied, as it ought to be by us or by the enemy soon. I advise you to send a brigade and hold it if we are to remain here."

Ewell peers across the green summer fields, toward the wooded hill which showed no evidence of occupation by the enemy.

"Are you sure it commands the town?" He asks.

"Certainly it does," says Trimble, becoming more and more impatient, "and it ought to be held by us at once."

Ewell was also growing impatient with his old friend and makes some comment to that effect. There is an uneasy moment of silence.

Trimble: "Give me a brigade and I will engage to take that hill."

No answer from Ewell.

"Give me a good regiment and I will do it!" Lee's words rushed through his mind: *throw an overwhelming force on their advance...drive one corps back on another....follow up the successes...*

Ewell shakes his head and looks through his glasses again.

Trimble storms away. He would not, under any circumstances, serve under such an officer!

* * *

Ewell's temporary headquarters at the house north of town was like a beehive. Aides, scouts, cavalrymen, staff couriers, all galloping up on lathered, panting horses, leaping from saddles, or lowering themselves jauntily like southern gentlemen coming back from the hunt. Colonel Smead rides up with a report from General Early: Johnson should move against Culp's Hill as soon as possible—it commands the Union position. That information should have sounded familiar to Ewell by now; it was what Trimble had been trying to tell him.

There was also a report from "Extra Billy" Smith that the Yankees were advancing upon Ewell's flank and rear down the York Road. Early was checking that report out, and probably swearing mightily for having to do so. Ewell to an aide: "Bring Early to me in a hurry!" The aide gallops off.

When Early arrives he recounts his recommendation to take Culp's Hill before the enemy does— and Ewell must be getting weary of the same thing over again—the hill with the cemetery would probably fall too, since the Yankees are whipped and Culp's Hill commands it. Lieutenant Smith: Ride to General Lee; tell him we can take the hill if supported on the right.

Major Walter Taylor of Lee's personal staff rides up. The commanding general sends his compliments and thinks it necessary only to press "those people" to gain the heights. Ewell, if possible, is to do this.

Smith returns from Lee (he and Taylor apparently passed each other on their respective missions) with the information that the troops to support Ewell's attack were not on the battlefield as of yet, but the commanding general wishes Ewell to take the cemetery if possible. Lee would be over soon to confer.

Ewell has a dilemma: Take the hill, "if possible", without expecting support on the right. Possibly Yankees advancing upon his left rear. His troops' momentum has been slowed by their passage through the town. All his subordinates want him to attack. But it is not they who will take the responsibility if the attack should fail and a lot of men get killed. Lee left it up to him—"if possible". Ewell waits, while the Union Army rests itself on the hill to his south and waits for their reinforcements just a few miles away, marching inexorably toward Gettysburg. For the first time in the battle the circumstances work against the Confederates, and an action that could bring them victory never takes place.

* * *

Late in the evening of July 1st, J. E. B. Stuart's troopers are in Carlisle, about 30 miles north of Gettysburg. Here he finds Union troops sent from Harrisburg to fall upon the Confederate left flank—Ewell's men—at Gettysburg. Stuart virtually immobilizes them by setting the U. S. Cavalry Barracks on fire and destroying their supplies. It is in Carlisle that he finally receives information and orders from the main army: Concentration is at Gettysburg. And so, he turns his back on the burning barracks, and urges his wretched troopers along one more forced march to Gettysburg.

* * *

There is some interesting correspondence from General Halleck in Washington to his subordinate General Meade with the Army of the Potomac that spans the day of July 1st. At 10:45 a.m., before Halleck could have received word that a battle was raging in southern Pennsylvania, he telegraphs Meade: "...The movements of the enemy yesterday indicate his intention to either turn your left, or to come himself by the South Mountain and occupy Cumberland Valley. Do not let him draw you too far to the east."

And later in the day, at 9:15 p.m., after Halleck has heard that a battle is under way:

"...Your tactical arrangements for battle seem good, so far as I can judge from my knowledge of the character of the country; but in a strategic view, are you not too far east, and may not Lee attempt to turn your left and cut you off from Frederick? Please give your full attention to his suggestion...."

To interpret: Frederick was Meade's base of supply, and, at this point in time, his main line of communication and retreat back to Washington should he be defeated or the capital be threatened by Confederates. Halleck was remembering, no doubt, Chancellorsville, but on a larger scale. At Chancellorsville the flanking move was merely tactical—designed to win a battle. Here, any flank movement could become strategic—in other words, affect the course of the war. Perhaps Halleck was also remembering his *Jomini* from West Point: "...as armies have been destroyed by strategic operations without the occurrence of pitched battles..."

* * *

July 2, 1863

"The enemy is there, and I am going to strike him."

—R. E. Lee

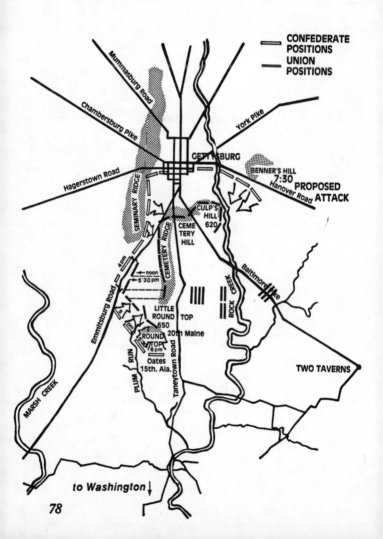

Battle of Gettysburg
July 2, 1863

CONFEDERATE POSITIONS
UNION POSITIONS

Mummasburg Road
Chambersburg Pike
York Pike
GETTYSBURG
Hagerstown Road
BENNER'S HILL
7:30 Hanover Road PROPOSED ATTACK
SEMINARY RIDGE
CULP'S HILL 620
CEMETERY HILL
CEMETERY RIDGE
Baltimore Pike
4pm
noon
5:30 pm
Emmitsburg Road
LITTLE ROUND TOP 650
20th Maine
ROCK CREEK
ROUND TOP 6pm
Oates 15th. Ala.
PLUM RUN
Taneytown Road
TWO TAVERNS
MARSH CREEK
to Washington ↓

78

Historians will ponder for years to come, why didn't Ewell seize Culp's Hill when he had the chance? And they will emphasize the fact that if he had, he would have captured an eminence from which his artillery could dominate the enemy position of Cemetery Hill and render it untenable, just as Trimble, Early, and finally Lee had seen. If Ewell had pressed the attack to Culp's Hill, and then extended his lines a mere 300 yards, he would have cut across the Baltimore Pike, the retreat route of the part of the Union Army now at Gettysburg. In essence, he would have driven a wedge between the battle-weary Union troops already on Cemetery Hill, and the march-weary Union troops coming up the Baltimore Pike from Maryland to reinforce those on Cemetery Hill.

There are reasons enough for Ewell not to have attacked: "Extra Billy" Smith's report of the enemy on his flank; Lee's ambiguous orders; the disorganization and loss of momentum his troops suffered while moving through the town in pursuit of the Yankees. But surely, more than one Confederate soldier, after hearing Union soldiers felling trees on Culp's Hill (after *they* occupied it) to build breastworks and clear fields of fire, and digging rifle-pits through the night of July 1, asked himself the question, "What if....?"

* * *

Longstreet was awake at 3:30 on the morning of July 2nd. After breakfast, he rode through the cool pre-dawn to find his commander Robert E. Lee. On the ridge overlooking the town where the Seminary Buildings were grouped, he found him. It was about 5:00 a.m.

From the beginning it was apparent that Lee and Longstreet were not planning the coming battle along the same lines. Longstreet renewed his proposal for a flank movement of some kind—certainly not another attack against what he had already expressed as a formidable position held by the Union Army. Lee merely said that he intended to attack. As events show, Longstreet was more upset about this than he let on at the moment.

Major General Lafayette McLaws arrives at the head of his division to report that his men are ready for battle. He is to become a pawn in the controversy between Lee and Longstreet.

Time passes as Lee waits for his scouts to come back with information concerning the terrain over which he intends to attack and the Union troop strength in that area. A party under Colonel Long of Lee's staff and General Pendleton, his chief of artillery, had already been in that area and had looked around, but Lee sent an engineer, Captain S. R. Johnston and a small party to reconnoiter for specifics. When they returned with their report, it was surprising in its content.

Johnston found Lee sitting upon a fallen log with a map across his knees. Johnston reported that he and his party had reached the small hill on the extreme left flank of the Union Army—Little Round Top—and found no troops. In fact, he said he had climbed to the summit and had found no enemy anywhere around. To Lee, this meant he could push an attack force up the Emmitsburg Road against the flank of the Union Army, which must lie somewhere north of Little Round Top without exposing the right flank of the attacking force to danger. Lee's mind was made up.

He calls McLaws over to show him how he wants the attack to be made—perpendicular to the Emmitsburg Road, driving into the Union flank which he believed to be north of the Round Tops. He would send Captain Johnston with him as a guide.

Longstreet breaks in. No, General McLaws, you are to make your attack this way, and shows a position on the map exactly at right angles to the one Lee has just described—parallel to the Emmitsburg Road. Longstreet either fears a flank attack from the area north of the Round Tops, or is merely being adamant, stalling, hoping that Lee will reconsider his plan of a flank march.

But Lee will have none of it. He corrects Longstreet and tells McLaws again that he wants his division placed perpendicular to the road. Longstreet takes the only course he can and forbids poor McLaws, who by now must feel caught between the wills of his two superiors, to leave his division and go with Johnston to reconoiter the area of attack.

Apparently, Longstreet calms down shortly after this outbust which gets him nowhere since Lee all but ignores it. He goes about assigning duties to his artillery, and Lee's plan is developed into an attack that will come later that day. The important thing to note is that Longstreet had in his mind an alternative to Lee's bludgeoning tactics. Both superb, intelligent officers—possibly the best in the country (if not the world) at the time, were disagreeing on a point of warfare.

It is more important than a mere clash of wills. It is, if we look at Longstreet's tactics, the birth of a new type of warfare, a maneuvering type of fighting rather than massive attack tactics. Swift, secret movement around the enemy, first used by Napoleon and propagated by the writings of Jomini, will be seen in battles yet to come, for at least a century. A "lightning war", if you will.

The conference was over. Lee had made up his mind to attack. He stood from the fallen log he had been seated on, mounted, and rode off to confer with

General Ewell on the disposition of his troops on the Confederate left to support Longstreet's assault. Longstreet stood and watched the commanding general ride off with his staff. Attack. Well, if that's what General Lee wants....

As Lee rode beyond sight, Longstreet turns to General Hood: "The General is a little nervous this morning; he wishes me to attack; I do not wish to do so without Pickett. I never like to go into battle with one boot off."

* * *

Both armies are in position. The Union Army lies in what is a fishook-shaped line—the barb of the hook on Culp's Hill, the curve of the hook running through the Cemetery, the straight shank running along the ridge that extends southward from the Cemetery, and the eye of the hook lying in the low ground just short of the two eminences known as Little Round Top and Round Top. The "Fishook" opens toward the south with three roads of major importance radiating out from it: the Emmitsburg Road back to Frederick and Washington; the Taneytown Road, also heading back toward Washington; and the Baltimore Pike, leading to Meade's base of supplies at Westminster, a railhead. The three roads are important because they are not only lifelines to the army—food, medical supplies, reinforcements, and communications flow up them—but they are also escape routes, should the Union Army be defeated, to alternate defensive positions closer to the capital of Washington. The advantage of this shape of line is that it is an "interior" line, meaning that troops can be shifted easily, along the inside of the curve, from one end of the line to the other for support against enemy attacks. The disadvantage, as seen by both Meade and Halleck, is its vulnerability to the south—where the hook opens, there are few troops to defend it. In military terminology, Meade's position can be flanked to the south.

The Confederate position outlines this fishook; east of Culp's Hill, running through the streets of Gettysburg, then southward along Seminary Ridge, a low ridge that runs parallel to and a mile distant from Cemetery Ridge. It is not a very good position for several reasons, the main one being that it is an "exterior" line, the opposite of the Union line with the drawback that troops must move around the rear of the line, in essence taking the long way, to support whichever end might be in danger. It would be a poor position to have to defend against attacks on the flanks.

Lee formulates his plan of battle for July 2. He will attack both ends of the Union line simultaneously. If he can keep both ends of the line busy, they cannot support each other. Timing is essential. Both ends of the enemy's line must feel threatened for the attack to be successful. Lee speaks to both his wing commanders, Ewell and Longstreet. Longstreet is to begin the attack against the southernmost end of the Union line. Ewell is to fake an attack on Culp's Hill, using lots of artillery at first. If it seems practicable, he is to develop this into a full scale attack.

* * *

J. E. B. Stuart's men were exhausted. They had ridden for nearly fifty hours straight to get to Gettysburg, escorting that cursed Yankee supply train. But they had done what they were supposed to do: they had harrassed the Union rear, drawing a couple of Yankee cavalry divisions after them; they had captured supplies, and, although the 125 wagons and uncooperative Yankee teamsters had slowed them down incredibly, they had reached the main army with the supplies for the seemingly ever-hungry men and horses of the Southern Army: they had captured what would amount to nearly a brigade of Blue cavalrymen, fought several pitched battles and won; set fire to the Carlisle Cavalry Barracks immobilizing the Union troops there with orders to sweep down on Lee's rear; all this at a cost of only 89 casualties.

They had had very little rest since the beginning. An hour or so of sleep when Stuart caught some of the men fallen asleep across the fence they were knocking down to pass their horses through. The men rested a little the afternoon and evening of July 2nd, grazed their horses with reins wrapped around their wrists and the trusted horses picking their way gently around their prostrate masters. But Stuart did not rest. He'd been through everything too, and it was harder for him because he also was carrying the burden of command. But it was different for him as well. He was not just a cavalryman. Nor was he just a cavalry commander, like Kilpatrick or Custer. He was J. E. B. Stuart, and that was the difference. While his men rested, he reported to Lee.

He rides up to Lee and his staff. Some of the staff look at him with impatience. Lee takes his eyes from his field glasses. "Well, General Stuart, you are here at last!"

The rebuke is puzzling. Reports will circulate later that Stuart did not support Lee the way he should have. But this is untrue. He followed orders as issued by Lee and approved by Longstreet. He hid Lee's movements from the enemy—Hooker did not attempt to cross the Potomac in pursuit of Lee until the 24th of June, nine days after the head of the Confederate column crossed the Mason-Dixon line and are in the North. Lee has had General Robertson's cavalry and Jones' squadrons to guard the passes in the Blue Ridge Mountains and his rear—3,000 cavalrymen under his direct orders. Ewell, the vanguard of the Confederate invasion had with him Jenkin's 1,800 troopers, and guarding the left of the Confederates were Imboden's cavalry—2,000 horses and men. If Stuart was shocked by Lee's comment he never reported it officially, nor made any mention that he was upset. But he should have been.

Still, as historians will, someday it will be said, "If only Lee had had Stuart's cavalry to guide him, he wouldn't have blundered into the Union Army at Gettysburg." The point is moot. Lee had all his troops concentrated before Meade did. You fight the enemy where you find him, and Lee found his enemy and whipped him badly on the first day of battle. He won the first day without Stuart, and now that he has Stuart, the question becomes instead of "Where have you been?" merely, "How do I use this cavalryman and his talents to their maximum?"

* * *

The men of Johnson's Division in Ewell's Corps are beginning to regret the fact that their commander had not taken the initiative yesterday to capture the hill in front of their position. Culp's Hill, in the sultry afternoon of July 2nd, now bristled with Union armaments. The Yankees have had time to entrench and clear fields of fire. Oh, it will be hell to pay to fight up the slope through the thick woods and into the fire from Yankees behind breastworks. Many a good Southern mother's heart will be broken because of a lost opportunity last evening.

With the old Stonewall Brigade at the base of Culp's Hill was a native Gettysburgian coming home for the first time in half a dozen years. Not only was he fighting now for the Confederate Army, but he was fighting on the very land that bore his family's name. Wesley Culp had come home to the family farm under most ironic circumstances.

Born in Gettysburg, Wesley Culp had grown up there, played in the woods and peaceful fields where he now dodged Yankee lead. Three years before the war broke out, he followed Mr. Hoffman, a carriage-maker, to Shepherdstown, Virginia.

In Shepherdstown he joined a local militia company called the Hamtramck Guards. It was an easy way for the stranger to make new friends—local militia outfits were more of a social organization in the South before the war than they were military units—and it was a time for socializing; Sunday afternoons spent drilling for the ladies in clean, pressed uniforms; picnics afterwards with pretty girls in their crinolines; talking about the impending doom of any Yankee who dares to set foot on Southern Soil....

And when the war broke out, the Hamtramck Guards rallied around the Confederate Battle-banner en masse. Wes went with them, thinking, like they all did, that the war could last but a few months, then they could all come back home heroes.

But the war dragged on making corpses of would-be heroes. Wesley Culp's Hamtramck Guards became Co. B, 2nd Virginia Infantry, in a brigade under the command of the awkward, eccentric ex-professor from Virginia Military Institute with the flame of genius flickering behind his bright blue eyes. Thomas J. Jackson won a name for his tenacity at First Manassas, and lent that name to his entire brigade. Though its commanders changed through the war, the Stonewall Brigade kept Jackson's nickname.

And now, the Stonewall Brigade and the young Gettysburgian who had finally come home, awaited orders to assault a position they could have leisurely walked to last night.

It seems as if the Union Army is not in a mood to attack. At least, its still untried commander of only four days is taking no chances. In this correspondence from Meade to Halleck, the commander of the Army of the Potomac attempts to assuage his senior's repeated fears of Lee flanking him:

July 2, 3:00 p.m.

"...If I find it hazardous to do so [meaning to attack] or am satisfied that the enemy is endeavoring to move to my rear and interpose between me and Washington, I shall fall back to my supplies at Westminster...."

* * *

While Longstreet is moving his troops into position on the Confederate right, Union General Daniel Sickles takes matters into his own hands. Without orders, he moves his entire Third Corps from its position below the Round Tops, to some higher ground near the Emmitsburg Road, closer to the Confederate line and, unknowingly, into the area across which Longstreet's assault will move.

Sickle's line forms an inverted "V"—stretching from a group of giant boulders called Devil's Den on his left below the Round Tops, to a Peach Orchard on the Emmitsburg Road, then bends back at a nearly 90 degree angle along the Emmitsburg Road, to end several hundred yards short of the rest of the Union line.

Meade is furious at Sickles when he discovers what he has done. Meade sees the tactical errors inherent in it: first, a "V" shaped line means that fire directed at the front of either side of the "V" will fall also into the rear of the other side, literally killing two "birds" with one stone; and second, he has left his right flank "in the air" with a giant gap between his troops and the rest of the Union Army through which Confederates could pour. Sickles offers to pull his troops back to their original position. A shell explodes nearby, almost striking Meade and Sickles. "Never mind," says Meade, "the enemy is about to save you the trouble!" and rides off to find reinforcements for Sickles.

It is 3:00 p.m. and Longstreet's artillery has opened on the Yankee line sitting on the top of the ridge by the Peach Orchard. After a half-hour cannonade, Longstreet's brigades sweep into action. In one of the most spirited assaults of the war, the Confederates drive the Union soldiers from their position near the Peach Orchard. The fighting swirls through the Wheatfield. The acre of wheat changes hands some six times, troops leaving bloody footprints where regiments fought and fell across the trampled wheat. The Confederate assault slows as they drive the Union troops back, true to Meade's prediction, to their original position and reinforcements.

* * *

Major General John B. Hood, as his division prepared itself for an attack on the Union position near the Peach Orchard, was not a happy man. Lee's orders, as passed to him through General Longstreet were to attack up the Emmitsburg Road. But the Union line, after Sickles' movement, was now in a position to do his troops a great deal of damage. If he were to attack into the area between the Peach Orchard and Devil's Den, driving along the Emmitsburg Road, he would be advancing his troops into a curved Union line which could lap around his flanks and kill many a Southern boy. In addition, some of his scouts had reported the large hill—Big Round Top—unoccupied, and with a clear path to a road—the Taneytown Road—where Union supply wagons were parked.

He sent an aide to General Longstreet with a request to alter his attack by moving his troops to the east, around Big Round Top. The messenger came back with the reply that General Lee's orders were to attack up the Emmitsburg Road. Hood sends another message, and again he receives the reply, "General Lee's orders are to attack up the Emmitsburg Road."

Finally, Hood goes himself to Longstreet, and receives no satisfaction: "We must obey the orders of General Lee."

A surprising turnaround for Longstreet. No doubt he can see merit in Hood's proposal since he had advocated the same type of maneuver twice before. Perhaps he is sulking, attempting to make certain, if this attack should fail, who would be to blame for its failure. We know by now that Lee is not fighting the battle the way Longstreet would fight it.

But Longstreet's sulkiness passes, because the maneuver is what he believes in—maneuver rather than attack, choose the ground to your advantage and await attack—it is the new type of warfare. He himself will propose a flanking maneuver again.

* * *

Brigadier General Evander M. Law's Brigade of Hood's Division of Longstreet's Corps had just completed a twenty-four mile march to the battlefield on the extreme right flank of the Confederate Army. Within Law's Brigade was the 15th Alabama Infantry Regiment, commanded by Colonel William C. Oates. They knew that they would be going into action soon, and their canteens were nearly dry, so Oates sent a detail with the canteens to the rear to bring back water.

Orders arrived before the canteens, and with only a brief rest, the Alabamians marched off again through the 80 degree heat of a July afternoon toward Round Top.

The ascent of Big Round Top was difficult—rocks and boulders, some the size of a small house, dot the incline; it is thickly wooded, nearly impossible for a regiment to pass through without breaking formation; and, behind those rocks and trees above them, Yankee sharpshooters.

The sharpshooters are swept away, but the heat and thirst are not. Oates' men reach the summit of Round Top and, without orders, all halt. Some have fainted from the heat, others are just exausted, but as a unit they rest, panting in the sultry woods.

Captain L. R. Terrill, General Law's assistant adjutant general, rides up and asks why Oates' men have halted. (No doubt he is cursed under the breath of many an enlisted man.) Oates, perhaps as an excuse, or perhaps to be polite to Law's adjutant, does not mention the obvious with men sprawled around. Instead, he suggests that Round Top, if it could be cleared, would be a fine place for artillery to command the Union line to the north of them. Terrill cannot change orders. The tactical advantages of this hill are of no concern to him; he is merely relaying orders to press on.

Oates gives the command and the 15th Alabama rises and moves off. They have spent maybe five minutes resting, but at this point, they may be the most important five minutes in the lifetime of the Confederacy.

Ahead of them, just across the little valley below Big Round Top is Little Round Top, a smaller but woodless hill which also commands the Union position. From it, artillery could sweep the Union line from its flank all the way to the Cemetery. And there would be no need to take time to clear the woods off of it—that was done the fall before by local farmers for firewood. It would also command the Taneytown Road, one of the Union Army's supply and retreat routes. And, while Oates' men had rested, it remained unoccupied by Union troops.

General G. K. Warren was an engineer with the Army of the Potomac, and, as such, had no combat troops under his command. After Meade had learned of Sickles' advance, he noticed that the eminence which commanded his left flank—Little Round Top—might have been left uncovered by Sickles' departure, and so sends General Warren to the hill to ascertain its importance, and any threat to it the enemy might present.

Warren rides to the summit of Little Round Top and is shocked. He can see the Confederate battleline sweeping around the back of Big Round Top and disappearing into the woods of the larger hill. And, what is worse, he finds himself, some Signal Corpsmen, and some orderlies the only Union soldiers on the hill. It all falls into place to Warren now, the tactical importance of this little hill that is the key to the Union position, and he sends couriers out with messages at a gallop, to bring troops—anyone's troops—to this hill on the double-quick!

Warren waits impatiently for what must have seemed an hour to him, expecting at any moment, the Confederates to come streaming off the side of Big Round Top and up the slope of Little Round Top.

He can wait no more, and goes off himself to find troops. In the meantime, Colonel Strong Vincent has intercepted a messenger at the base of Little Round Top and wheedles out of him the information that Little Round Top is to be occupied. Vincent immediately grasps the tactical importance of the hill, and without orders, puts his men in motion to seize it. It is a decision that will cost the 26 year old Colonel his life in the fighting that is to come. As

Vincent's men begin their ascent of Little Round Top, Oates' Confederates are rising from their exaustion in the stifling woods of Big Round Top, grumbling and getting into line to prepare to advance.

The fighting on the slopes of Little Round Top is vicious, with Oates' Confederates trying to work their way around the Union left flank with each assault. The Union soldiers in that area were outnumbered almost two to one, but they had the advantage of defense—squatting behind boulders and trees above the Confederates—and also the advantage of having Joshua Chamberlain for a commander.

Chamberlain was an ex-seminarian who had given up the black cloth of the ministry for the blue cloth of arms. He is wounded twice within a few minutes of placing his men in position on the extreme left flank of the entire Union Army, but the wounds are minor compared to the importance of the ground his regiment holds. As Oates' men slide farther and farther around to Chamberlain's left, he responds by altering his line—bending his left flank back and stretching the men out more thinly than they already are.

Chamberlain (and Oates too, no doubt) can hear the severity of the fighting to the west, just a few yards around the curve of the slope of Little Round Top. The fighting there seemed to be going in favor of the Union troops. But here, the Confederates just kept coming on, assault after assault. Then, in a lull, Chamberlain hears it: the call from his men, "Ammunition!" "Yes, here too." And from the other end of the line as well, "Ammunition!"

It must have been an eerie, welcome sound to the Confederates, who no doubt heard it, being no more than fifty yards away. Though they could not see their enemy through the trees and the haze of battle, the sound of men calling for ammunition meant it was time to take their position away from them. Oates' men began their advance.

Chamberlain knew his men had already robbed their dead and wounded of ammunition. They were indeed, out of ammunition. There was only one thing to do. His men pondered the desperate situation before them, but Chamberlain had no doubts. "Fix bayonets!" he orders through the haze.

Those who had them fixed bayonets; those who didn't grabbed the barrels of their muskets, club-like. The order to attack was given, and attack they did.

It was the last thing the Confederates expected, to see wild-eyed, musket-swinging men swarming down from the side of the hill they had clung so tenaciously to for so long. The shock effect worked. Confederates reeled back before the onslaught of Chamberlain's men. Confederates ran back toward Big Round Top and down the valley between Big and Little Round Top to Devil's Den, Yankees chasing them almost as if it were some childlike game.

Chamberlain's troops halted. With one incredible gamble, this theologian turned warrior had defended the most tactically important piece of terrain on the battlefield from Confederate occupation. He had saved the Union left flank and rear from the enemy, and denied the South its second chance for victory in the battle.

* * *

"General Lee, my scouts have found a way around the flank and rear of the enemy," said Longstreet.

"General, you had no orders to send out scouts. You know of my intentions for an assault upon the Union center as soon as Pickett's Division is up."

"Yes, General, but I cannot allow you to pursue your plans for a frontal assault without considering other more prudent possibilities." He would press the issue again. He would press it until Lee understood what he was trying to say or be relieved of his command for insubordination. These boys were too good to kill.

"General Longstreet, the enemy is there and I am going to strike him."

"Do you not trust my judgement as much as you trusted Jackson? He proposed just such a flank march less than two months ago at Chancellorsville and it won us our greatest victory yet. But it did not end this damnable war because we were still in our own back yards. What I propose now will end it."

Something in Lee moved at that moment. The pains in his chest, the anger at Stuart, the disappointment with Ewell, the burden of two years of warfare suddenly seemed to lift as he looked into Longstreet's fierce, bearded, warrior's face. Yes, he thought. This was the look that Jackson had had of determination, confidence, conviction, the night before his march into the Union flank at Chancellorsville. This was the look Napoleon must have had before Marengo, thought Lee. Or Hannibal before Rome. Or the Duke of Wellington before Waterloo....

"Yes, General Longstreet. Come sit down with me. What is your plan?"

* * *

The fighting on the Union left flank was drawing additional Union troops like a magnet. To bolster up this threatened end of the Union line, Meade was pulling troops from other sections of his line, including the Culp's Hill sector.

While Ewell's Confederate artillery dueled with some Union guns on East Cemetery Hill, a good portion of the Union Army's 12th Corps was put into motion toward the southern area of the battlefield, to help Sickles out of his predicament. They left their entrenchments unmanned.

Close to 7:00 p.m., Ewell had decided that this diversion which Lee had ordered as part of Longstreet's assault should develop into a full-scale attack. It was a good decision, since the Union trenches, at least in part, had been vacated, and a mere 500 yards beyond them lay the Baltimore Pike. It would be an easy thing, (although Ewell didn't know it at this time) to capture the Union line, then advance to cut their supplies and communications, and generally throw their rear-guard on the Baltimore Pike into confusion. In essence, he could place his troops on the Baltimore Pike and be between the Union Army and one route back to the capital.

As Ewell was about to launch his men against the Union position on Culp's Hill, a courier gallops up with an urgent directive: *"Suspend action. Hold your present position. Do not attack until further orders are received. R. E. Lee, General."* For a third time, a Confederate assault that could bring them victory is halted.

* * *

IV. The Perfect Battle

"Young man, why did you not tell me that before the battle?...Even as stupid a man as I am can see it all now."

> —R. E. Lee, replying to a student of the Battle of Gettysburg after the war.

SPECIAL ORDERS   Hdqrs. Army of Northern Va,
NO. 176.   Gettysburg, Pa., July 2, 1863

I. General Stuart's Cavalry will march by way of the right flank of this army and, using whatever cover the ground offers so as to conceal his movements from the enemy, secure with his artillery the roads to Baltimore and Taneytown, leaving behind enough cavalry to guide and protect the column of infantry which will follow.

II. General Ewell's Corps will withdraw from its present position, leaving behind a sufficient number of troops to maintain campfires and keep up a diversionary fire against the enemy. They will march by way of the town, behind our present lines along the west side of the ridge so as to conceal their movements from the enemy, following the route as improved by General Stuart's march. They will take up positions across the road to Emmitsburg, generally following the high ground north of Marsh Creek. The men will immediately entrench and fortify their position with artillery along the Emmitsburg Road.

III. General Hill will follow with his Corps, behind the ridge, following the same route, then positioning his troops along the ridge that generally follows the road past St. Mark's Church, using the Rock Creek Plain to his defensive advantage. He will fortify his position by entrenching immediately and placing his artillery to cover the Taneytown Road.

IV. General Longstreet will march his Corps generally along the same route, using the roads behind the newly established line, and take up a position on the Rock Creek Plain in the vicinity of the road to Baltimore, with special attention given to fortifying the road to Baltimore with artillery.

V. The trains will follow moving by roads to Fairfield, thence along roads to the west of the army.

VI. This movement will be done with the utmost vigor and promptness. Silence will be maintained in all cases. No cheering or shouting will be allowed in ranks.

VII. The Army's base of operations will be changed to Fredericktown in Maryland.

VIII. All operations will be completed by noon, July 3, 1863.

By command of R. E. Lee, General:

W. H. Taylor,
Assistant Adjutant General

* * *

"The question is, sir, whom do we leave as a rear guard?" asked Ewell.

"Who else," replied Walker. "The old Stonewall Brigade." Ewell paused and thought about Jackson. Yes. It would have suited him to have his old brigade in such an important although desperate position.

"Then go to them, General, and prepare your lines."

* * *

As their comrades marched off, the men of Jackson's old command stoked the campfires. A dubious distinction, this, to be the rear guard. No doubt they would be captured as soon as the Yankees find out what was up. Then to prison: Elmira or Johnson's Island, maybe. But if this movement is successful, the boys might not have to spend too long in the hell-holes. Then again, there was one other alternative. How many times had they heard Old Jack himself say it. When General Bee rode up to him at First Manassas and told him that the Yankees were pushing his men back. What was he going to do? "Sir, we will give them the bayonet!" Surrender? No, Jackson would not have liked that. Better to die game. But with the war so close to being over. If they are only successful....

* * *

The men of Stuart's Cavalry slept restlessly through the hot afternoon—the uneasy sleep of near-total exhaustion. At eight p.m. on the second of July, McClellan, Stuart's trusted adjutant, touched the sleeping General on the shoulder, and Stuart was awake and in full command of his faculties—instantly—a scene that had been played enough times to attract praise from the Commanding General himself. McClellan handed Stuart Lee's order No. 176, and in the growing twilight, Stuart read that he was to lead Ewell's Corps around the rear of their army to a new position south of the Yankees. Fine. Wade Hampton will lead. If there is trouble ahead the South Carolinian can handle it. Fitz Lee and Chambliss follow. The men have had four or five hours rest, not counting time asleep in the saddle. That is enough. The horses have been fed and rested a bit. Let's move. The head of Ewell's column should be moving soon. No bugles, keep it quiet, send the couriers. Stuart wants to be in column and waiting for Ewell.

* * *

On the other side of the battlefield, blue-clad couriers galloped out in the darkness, found their assigned Generals, snapped salutes and spoke their message: "General Meade sends his regards and requests the honor of your presence at a meeting of Corps Commanders. If you'll just follow me, sir, I will conduct you to headquarters...."

One by one they rode up to the small cottage on the side of the road to Taneytown, and dismounted. It was just before 9:00 p.m. The night air had begun to cool things off a little. In the distance, over by Culp's Hill, some firing could still be heard.

Inside the little house, in the front room not more than 12 feet square, it was hot and stuffy. Insects were drawn to the flickering oil lamps and candles, and the shadows of the officers who were to decide the fate of the United States danced across the walls.

They were all there, and began trading stories of the day's fighting, like athletes after a game. "You should have seen my second division. They were whipped, but fought like devils all the way back. Finally stopped the rebels at our old line. You can push those boys just so far, and then...." They talk of casualties, seemingly a badge of honor, whose corps lost the most. General Birney, in command after Sickles' wounding, expressed the feeling that his corps, the third, was pretty much used up to be of too much further use. Sickles' rashness had cost them plenty. No one knew that better than General Meade, who had been with Sickles when the rebels attacked his untenable position at the Peach Orchard.

Only Warren did not participate. Overcome by the heat of the day, wounded, in shock, and exhausted, he slumped down in a corner and promptly fell asleep.

They talked about supplies. There were plenty back in Westminster, the base of supplies, but perhaps only one more day's worth with the army. So the generals assumed. Deep down inside they knew that the men had probably cooked and eaten all their three day's rations on the first day, but were probably capable of "foraging" ("stealing" to the local farmers who were victimized) enough food for at least a couple more days.

General Butterfield, Chief of Staff, kept notes. The generals totalled up their best estimates of troop strengths. Butterfield recorded 58,000.

Military alternatives were discussed. Attack or defend? How is the position now occupied compared with a position that might be found closer to the base of supplies? Finally, General Newton pipes up. He states emphatically that this is no place to fight battle.

General Gibbon, junior officer present (since Warren is asleep) is astounded, but nevertheless interested. Newton's reputation as an engineer is formidable. He asks Newton to explain.

His objections were simple enough. They could be flanked to the south. Lee, he said, was certainly not fool enough to attack the Union center after the fighting on the flanks had compacted the army into a strong position.

A flank march by Lee. It was becoming his trademark. If anyone in that room thought that, it was Howard, whose men had been humiliated by Stonewall Jackson's flank attack just two months before, almost to the day, at Chancellorsville. Meade may have thought about the telegraphic messages he had received the day before from "Old Brains" Halleck warning about his position and the possibility of Lee flanking him.

Meade expressed concern about the irregular shape of his line. Although the fish-hook shape gave him an interior line allowing excellent communications between all parts of the army, perhaps a straighter line would be better. The old Pipe Creek Line is brought up, and the accompanying withdrawal into Maryland should the Pipe Creek Line be sought is discussed.

Butterfield interrupts. He presents three questions and suggests that they vote on them.

The generals listen, straining over the distant firing on Culp's Hill to hear Meade's Chief of Staff.

First: "Under existing circumstances, is it advisable for this army to remain is its present position, or to retire to another nearer its base of supplies?" All present agree that they should stay. Gibbon, Newton, and Hancock suggest that the position of the army must be corrected.

Second: "It being determined to remain in present position, shall the army attack or await attack by the enemy?" All vote to await attack. Newton says by all means do not attack. Hancock says to wait, unless of course, their communications with Washington are cut. Only if they are flanked should they attack.

Third: "If we await attack, how long?" Most of the officers think one day should be long enough. Newton, once again expresses worry that if they wait it will give Lee time to cut their communications with Washington, their route to their base of supplies at Westminster, and their retreat routes back to their capital.

General Slocum is asked his opinion. On each question he replies that they should "stay and fight it out."

"Such then is the decision," says Meade. The Council of War is adjourned.

Gibbon approaches Meade, as the small group disintegrates into the darkness, and says he is confused. Why, he asks, was he, a division commander, invited to a meeting of Corps commanders.

"That is all right," says Meade. "I wanted you here. If Lee attacks tomorrow, it will be on your front."

"Why do you think so?" asked the grizzled junior officer.

"Because he has made attacks on both our flanks and failed, and if he concludes to try it again it will be on our center."

"I hope he does," says Gibbon. "If he does, we will most definitely defeat him."

* * *

And so the orders were received and read with interest. Ewell's Corps began its march at 9:00 p.m. under the cover of darkness, leaving a rear guard of three regiments of Walker's Brigade, still called, with no small amount of pride, "The Stonewall Brigade." They would demonstrate along with a battery on Benner's Hill behind them, firing occasionally and keeping the line of campfires flickering through the night.

The flanking maneuver was done by "peeling back" the brigades farthest from the right flank of the Confederate line—in this case, the brigades of Ewell's Corps first—and marching them behind the rest of the army. Care was taken to use the woods and declivities in the terrain to hide their movement until they reached the town and the screen of the houses. The battery on Benner's Hill and the infantry rear guard kept up such a racket that most of the Confederates were happy to be withdrawing. Confusion was evident in some whispered conversations. "Why," was the question, "the orders for silence?" "Why the diversion from the guns?" The officers knew, but told no one. It was an all too rare occurrence where orders were issued so quickly and effectively that they preceeded even camp rumor.

They moved through the darkness, fifty minutes marching, ten minutes rest, covering (as Jackson himself had calculated once) two miles in that time span. Citizens of the town stared out the windows of darkened houses and wondered where these ragged men were headed now.

* * *

Wesley Culp was having the strangest night of his life. First, fighting a battle in his own backyard, or practically, since it was his uncle's farm where they had done the fighting earlier today, and now, marching into the town, past his old house, along the streets where he had rolled his hoop as a child, and run errands down, and later rode away to follow the carriage trade to Shepherdstown, Virginia. He'd seen his sister Anna and Julia just last night and promised that he'd come back as soon as he had the chance. Now what? How long would it be before he'd have another chance to see his family again if the army was retreating. Maybe never.

* * *

The route, at first, was not difficult to follow. The giant, undulating animal that was the Confederate Army, snaked its way through the square of Gettysburg, out the road to Chambersburg, over the crest of the ridge where the Seminary buildings stood, then turned abruptly left to cut through the fields behind the ridge. There they linked up with Stuart's Cavalry who took the lead.

For three and a half hours they marched, below the backbone of the ridge, concealed from the Union position. Looking to the left they could see their own troops—Hill's and Longstreet's men—their campfires flickering in the darkness. Not a word was passed, no shout, no jeer, no sound between the lines. Everyone had gotten word.

It was a few minutes past one o'clock in the morning when the head of the column struck the road to Emmitsburg. Now things should go much smoother. No plowed fields to traverse, no woods to pick their way around. Thank God for the nearly full moon that shone brightly between occassional scudding clouds.

By two-thirty they found themselves at Greenmount—nothing more than a Post Office building—and found themselves also with the realization that they were not retreating. At a small dirt road just before the bridge over Marsh Creek, they turned left. The buzz among the men was audible. A flanking movement! By God, we're going around them again!

* * *

It is a ghostly dance that the column of cavalry puts on as they wind their way ahead of Ewell's Corps along the west side of Seminary Ridge. The columns undulates, since there is no road to follow back there, but the movement forward is inexorable. Videttes are out, though they can expect no trouble until they hit the road to Emmitsburg. There are probably Yankees there, but they won't be expecting a large column of enemy cavalry in the middle of the night. The thought of capturing them without a fight crosses Stuart's mind, but knowing Hampton, he'll probably want a fight. Stuart sends a galloper to Hampton with a message to avoid firing if he can. Stuart would go himself, but the men might cheer. At this point they need silence. The cheers can come later.

* * *

July 3, 1863

*"It may be laid down as a general prin-
ciple that the decisive points of
maneuver are on that flank of the
enemy upon which, if his opponent
operates, he can more easily cut him
off from his base and supporting
forces without being exposed to the
same danger."*

—Jomini

If the South Won Gettysburg

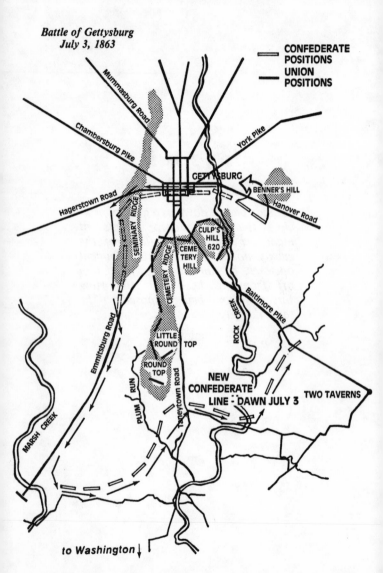

Battle of Gettysburg
July 3, 1863

CONFEDERATE POSITIONS
UNION POSITIONS

Mummasburg Road

Chambersburg Pike

York Pike

GETTYSBURG

BENNER'S HILL

Hagerstown Road

Hanover Road

SEMINARY RIDGE

CEMETERY RIDGE

CULP'S HILL 620

CEMETERY HILL

Baltimore Pike

ROCK CREEK

Emmitsburg Road

LITTLE ROUND TOP

ROUND TOP

PLUM RUN

Taneytown Road

NEW CONFEDERATE LINE - DAWN JULY 3

TWO TAVERNS

MARSH CREEK

to Washington ↓

It turned out the way it nearly always had at the beginning of the war. A single Union Cavalry vidette on the road catching just a glimpse of mounted figures coming out of the moonlit darkness. A call for the password. No answer. The Yankee spinning his horse to head back and warn the main force of something amiss, and then there they were behind him— more enemy horsemen between him and the rest of his outfit.

Hampton's men had all but surrounded the 6th U. S. Cavalry on the Emmitsburg Road before they knew it. A few escaped, firing as they went. That's all right though, thought Hampton. They'll find their way back to Headquarters too late to do anything. And there had been sporadic firing all night anyway. The important thing is that they had captured most of them, avoided a time consuming battle, and didn't tip off the rest of the Yankee Army with a lot of firing south of their main line. The infantry followed Hampton's men, passing the still flickering Yankee Cavalry campfires and the dishevelled and sleepy-eyed Yankee troopers sitting ignominiously before them.

* * *

The officers went about preparing the lines. The ground to the north of the creek was almost ideal for defense. The Emmitsburg Road sector had two small hills that did not show up on Hotchkiss' map. They were cleared and artillery was placed on them, thereby commanding the road past Greenmount that led to Emmitsburg and eventually to Frederick. Ewell placed a brigade on the sloping plain to the south of Marsh Creek straddling the road. As long as the creek didn't rise five feet, it was fordable at almost any point. He could support this brigade with the rest of his line and protect it with the artillery behind, and the creek would be an obstacle to any Union forces trying to attack the position.

From the Marsh Creek crossing, the line ran along the ridge, then crossed Rock Creek at the bridge on the road to Taneytown. Once again the small rises were fortified with artillery which commanded the bridge and swept the road. The line then turned a little northward and ran along the Rock Creek plain. The plain in this area reminded some of the men of Malvern Hill—a barren, open field of fire in most places—but different because it had a creek at its base. Just deep enough so that anyone crossing it would have to hold musket and cartridge box high over the swirling water, and, of course, expose themselves to fire without being able to fire back.

The Baltimore Pike was masterpiece of defense. Along the sides of the road were lined the guns of Longstreet's artillery—not facing straight down the road, but angled so as to criss-cross their fire, so that any troops advancing up the road would come under a latticework of deadly missles. The right flank was secured by a heavy concentration of guns from Dearing's battalion. The men worked into the late afternoon clearing a field of fire on the plain that led down to White Run, a tributary of Rock Creek.

The rear of the line was a web of roads—communications between the flanks of the army were set up easily. The Army's base of supply was being switched to Frederick in Maryland. From Frederick, a railroad ran to the Shenandoah Valley, the "Breadbasket" of the South and a source of nearly limitless supplies.

The roads were secured. The men dug in. The Confederate Army of Northern Virginia was squarely between the Union Army and the capital of Washington, D.C. All they had to do now was wait.

* * *

"General Meade, Sir, something is terribly wrong!" It was nearing dawn. Meade had just closed his eyes after the Council of War and riding the lines personally to prepare for the attack he was certain would come sometime on the 3rd. Now this.

"Yes, Captain. What seems to be the problem?"

"I don't know where to begin, Sir. Kilpatrick has just come in with a report that the Confederates are not in position. They seem to have left a rear-guard near the town—a very strong rear-guard that doesn't seem to want to retire as it should. They appear to be barricading the town. The rest of the army has retired. Some stragglers from the 6th U. S. Cavalry came in last night and reported a sharp fight out on the road to Emmitsburg with Stuart. Some of them said that they thought the rebels were heading out that road. If they are retiring, I don't know why they're going that way. They should be heading toward the mountains, Sir. And the rear-guard should be retiring, not holding on. I just don't understand it, Sir."

Meade sat on his cot as all this rolled out of the adjutant. What was Lee up to now? How could he do it? How could he know his opponents so well as to predict what they would do nearly every time? McClellan, Pope, Burnside, Hooker. But not me, thought Meade. I will not take him for granted.

Now, thought Meade, what is the worst possible thing he could do? Attack? No, he's done that for two days now. Retreat? Possibly, to find a better position farther north, to threaten Harrisburg again and draw me away from...Washington. Washington! That's why he is moving southward, why he struck the road to Emmitsburg. Oh, my God! He's flanking me! He's striking south to get between our army and Washington!

He sat there speechless. It's probably too late to even do anything now. He's stolen a night's march on us. While we were in our Council of War last night deciding to stay where we were and await his attack, he was deciding not to attack. He knew what we were going to do in our caution, and what we expected him to do, and he did the opposite. A wry smile crossed Meade's face now. He smiled because he had just been part of the perfect maneuver, the kind of thing that will be written up for students in Tactics classes at the Point to read about in years to come, as he—and Lee—had read about Cannae, and Marathon, and Waterloo. It was an appreciatory smile because of the strange feeling he had that he was witness to a genius at work.

"Sir?" The adjutant, awaiting orders and wondering why his commanding general was in such a good mood upon hearing this peculiar move of the enemy.

All right, thought Meade, beginning now to play the game of wills that war is, Lee's gotten around us. Or has he? Depending upon when he started his march. That damned rear-guard over on the right—that was the firing they had heard at the Council of War. I wonder if the maneuver is complete by now? I wonder if he's made it?

"Captain, I want cavalry to head out the Baltimore Road. Back them up with some of the Sixth Corps. I want a reconnaisance in force. Immediately. I need information as quickly as possible." It might not be too late, if they could secure the road to Baltimore before Lee does.

"Yes, Sir." The young aide turned to walk out. "Sir, do you know what the enemy is up to?"

Meade looked at the youthful adjutant, the

smile now replaced by a tiredness. "Yes, son. I know what he's up to. He's whipping us. He's winning the battle right before our eyes."

* * *

The checklist was nearly complete: Roads to Baltimore, Taneytown, and Emmitsburg secured with heavy emplacements of artillery; the men were still digging in even though it was just after noon. The Yankees must surely know by now what has happened. There was some desultory firing over by Longstreet's lines earlier this morning—probably the Yankees finding out that their retreat routes were being cut. When that information gets back to headquarters, they must certainly attack, and soon. Their communications with Washington are dead, except for perhaps a trickle of information going by courier out the road to Hanover. Washington must be in a panic, J. E. B. Stuart is thinking. Well, if they aren't by now, maybe we can give them something to worry about.

Stuart sends a request to General Lee: His troopers are a little tired (an incredible concession, considering J. E. B. Stuart!), they need just a little rest. But early tomorrow, may they raid the Northern Capital?

The reply is swift from General Lee: If you can leave enough cavalry to cover the flanks and the lines of communications and supply to Frederick, you may strike at Washington.

Stuart makes sure that the horse artillery had extra ammunition. No seige against Washington, but certainly an artillery bombardment of the Capitol Building. If they move swiftly enough, who knows how much damage they can do? The men and horses will still be tired, but when they learn that they are headed toward Washington, that should buoy their spirits! The defenses of Washington must be pretty well stripped. If they are not, we don't have to attack, but merely stay close enough to them to protect the rear of the main army here. Stuart's information concerning the Union troops at Frederick was that they are thinly spread along the lines of communication. Imboden should be able to handle that. Lee can have all the cavalry but Fitzhugh Lee, Chambliss, and Hampton. He must take Hampton, thought Stuart. How the former congressman from South Carolina will love to shell his old place of employment!

Now that they are in place in the rear of the Union Army and dug in, it seems like such a simple thing. The infantry must hold, but there should be no question about that. What was it Jackson used to say? "My men sometimes fail to take a position, but they never fail to defend one." That Jackson were alive to see this!

* * *

Unfortunately for Meade, the Confederates had not yet cut his communications with Washington. It would have been better if they had, so that Lincoln and Stanton and Halleck could not have heard the news. That it has happened again; that Lee has out-maneuvered, out-thought, out-generalled yet another Union commander. But the line through Hanover still clicked its staccatto death-knell: We are flanked to the south. We will change position to meet the attack of the enemy. If he does not attack today, we will be compelled to attack tomorrow.

Meade was going to recommend that the capital was in danger of attack, and that all efforts should be made to reinforce the defenses around Washington, but he knew that the defenses had been weakened nearly to the breaking point by Hooker's and his own requests for more troops as he followed the Confederates northward during the month of June. He could also suggest that they ease the seige of Vicksburg so as to evoke a much gentler attack or perhaps none at all, if negotiations could be struck up, but that would all be for Halleck and Lincoln to figure out. He would communicate only what is of military importance.

* * *

Chandler, in the telegraph office in Washington, leaped to his feet. He couldn't be hearing this right! He had to have read it wrong. They will repeat it. Listen closer, he told himself.

Major Eckert was behind him now. *He* would have to give the message to the President, thought the young telegrapher, because *I* am surely not! Here it comes again: "....flanked to the south....compelled to attack..." The rebels between Meade and Washington! How did they do it?

Halleck was wild, shouting orders and directions in between cursing Meade and Lee and Stanton. The key's clicking doubled as everything but the curses began to flow toward Meade. Change position, attack by all means, do not, repeat, do not wait until tomorrow. Attack immediately before Lee has time to entrench or attack Washington. Drive him from his position at all costs.

* * *

Jefferson Davis read the telegrapher's report and smiled. Immediately he sent a message to General Pemberton in Vicksburg:

> War Department
> Richmond, Va. 11:00 a.m.
> July 3.

General Pemberton:
Lee has maneuvered around the enemy's flank at Gettysburg, Pa. after two days battle there. Finds himself now between them and their capital. Hold out at all costs. Repeat, hold on to lines at Vicksburg

at all costs. Expect Washington to sue for peace shortly.

Jeff. Davis.

"This message must go through as quickly as possible," Davis said to his telegrapher. "It must get through."

"I will send it through General Johnston's Army. Our communications with them have been good up until just recently. And Johnston has been in communication with General Pemberton frequently."

"Fine. Just so long as he holds out a few more days."

* * *

Chandler had never seen so much confusion in the telegraph office before. Lincoln was pacing frantically, and had asked him at least a dozen times in the last hour if there had been any word from Meade—as if he wouldn't tell the President the moment the box started spelling out "Washington." Stanton was there, stroking his long beard as if to wrench it from his face. Halleck's already bulging eyes were practically popping out of their sockets. Only Major Eckert remained relatively unaffected, consumed with the business of running the office.

But there was only a trickle of information at the moment. It had been that way for the last several hours. The rebels, on the invasion, had destroyed all the wire from Gettysburg to Hanover. Up until now, all communications were coming by courier to Hanover, thence to Hanover Junction, and then southward to Washington. The problem was in the courier. So much to go wrong with a man riding messages to and fro. And with the way Stuart has been acting on this campaign, there was no telling what would happen.

"General, what are the dispositions of the other large armies in the field?" asked the Commander-in-Chief.

Halleck thought for just a moment. "General Rosecrans is in Tennessee with his army..."

Too far away, thought Lincoln.

"General Gillmore is now in command of the Department of the South near Charleston, South Carolina..."

And could never make it to Washington in time...

"Grant, of course, is..."

"At Vicksburg." Lincoln finished the sentence for Halleck.

"General Halleck, then where are the nearest troops to Washington?"

"French's troops, from Harper's Ferry. They evacuated the Ferry on the 27th or 28th, and are in Frederick City guarding the communications between Washington, Baltimore, and Meade."

"But since Lee is between the Army of the Potomac and Washington, there are no communications from that direction."

"Yes, but they are in the rear of Lee." said Halleck.

"How many troops does French have and what are their dispositions?" asked Lincoln.

"As of last report, he had about 7,000 troops, most of them strung out guarding the wires between Baltimore, Washington, and Frederick." Old Brains started thinking now. He saw what Lincoln was getting at now. Stuart probably has 6 or 7,000 cavalrymen with him, and he'd be a fool if he didn't make a raid on Washington. He could easily break through French's stretched-out line almost anywhere he chooses.

"Perhaps General French's troops would be of

more use as a defensive line before this city?" said Lincoln.

"No doubt," Stanton butted in. The relations between Halleck and Stanton were nearly at the breaking point now. Halleck ignored the insinuation with nothing more than a look towards the Secretary of War. He turned to Chandler.

"Send this to General French: Fall back on Washington immediately, taking care to...."

His voice trailed off. Lincoln looked at Stanton.

"Mr. Stanton, the situation reminds me of a friend I had once in Springfield...."

"Mr. President, please! I don't think I could stand one of your little stories right now. If you'll excuse me, I must go. We happen to be losing the war right before your eyes. I'll be in my office. I have been here too long already."

Chandler saw Stanton stalk out the door to his office and slam it behind him. So this is how it happens, he thought. He looked at the order he had just copied from Halleck's revised dictation and began to cipher it toward Frederick:

Washington D.C.
July 3, 1863

Major-General French
Frederick, Md.:

The Commander-in-Chief orders you to consolidate your troops before this city as quickly as possibly to contest any movement against the capital that the enemy may make. It is hoped that you will complete this movement in as short a time as possible, since the enemy has a large number of cavalry at his immediate disposal.

Your line of defense should be somewhere in the vicinity of Rockville, or farther south as the terrain dictates. Please communicate.

> Major-General Halleck,
> General-in-Chief

Halleck suddenly remembered a phrase he had learned once in grade-school latin. It impressed him because it had something to do with history and the military. And now, almost ominously, it came back to him. "Hannibal ante portas." Hannibal before the gates. The gates of Rome. "Lee before the gates." Will that phrase be taught to school children two-thousand years from now, he thought?

* * *

Warren was back. His report to General Meade of the terrain in front of the Confederate position was not optimistic. Open plains, a stream to cross, the Confederates mostly dug into the side of the plain in prepared rifle-pits. They've certainly taken advantage of the time they've won. When did they ever sleep? he wondered to himself. No report as of yet about the practicability of an attack being launched against their flank. They definitely have all the roads covered. Kilpatrick had come back after his reconnaisance in force with Sedgewick's men down the road to Baltimore. They were there all right. Lee's line now stretched from the Emmitsburg Road—the road back to Washington—to the Baltimore Road. He was squarely between the Union Army and the Capital.

Well, an attack must be made immediately. Meade had received his orders from Halleck. Old Brains wants an attack. A rash decision, thought Warren, without even seeing the terrain. Things must be getting worse in Washington.

After hearing Warren's report, Meade asked where Warren thought an attack would have the best chance of success. There was as uneasy silence in the headquarters.

"I'm not sure, General," said Warren. He did not want to make the decision that would literally send hundreds of men to eternity. He was an engineer, a staff officer; this responsibility should be on other shoulders. He hedged: "This sector is a little more wooded, and perhaps would afford a little more protection to the advancing troops."

"All right, then. I want General Hancock here. GO!" An orderly practically leaped from the little room to his horse outside.

"No. Stop him. This will never do. I will go see General Hancock myself." Meade rolled up the map and started for the door. "General Warren?"

Warren's head was downcast. He was distant. His mind was a thousand miles away. "Yes, sir." He picked up his gauntlets and followed Meade out the door.

* * *

Meade lost 1,100 men in the assault at dusk on the evening of the third. Confederate artillery swept the plain. Rifle fire from the pits was terrific. One young infantryman would remember the cries of the wounded through the night as they mixed with the sound of the pouring rain like a deep, macabre chorus of voices chanting "never.......forever..... never.......forever......."

It rained in torrents all through the night of the third and into the day of July 4th. Rock Creek overflowed its banks and many a mother's boy, though spared from death by being merely wounded in the attack, drowned in the current, too weak to move himself. Some Confederates crawled out, risking their lives to pull their enemies from a swirling death. No Yankee fired at them.

* * *

Stuart was with Generals Lee and Longstreet when Hancock's assault was repulsed. They had breached the line at one point, but Longstreet had thrown in parts of Pickett's Division, fresh from guarding wagon trains in the rear of the Army, and they plugged the gap and drove the Yankees back. Casualties were moderate for the Confederates, heavy for the Yankees, since they were fairly good targets moving up the open plain. Once again, Confederate officers, irrepresible in their thirst for combat, had taken heavy losses. Garnett was killed, perhaps, historians would speculate later, to prove to the army the unfairness of Stonewall Jackson's accusations of cowardice, a year before at Kernstown. He had been living and fighting more recklessly, it was noticed by those around him, since that affair. He was ill on the day of the Battle of Two Taverns (as this action of July 3rd, 1863, would be called in the South—the Battle of Rock Creek by the North) and rode his horse into the fight. Armistead was wounded in the action—just slightly—and was expected to recover. Kemper was also wounded most desperately. His fate was in limbo. These officers, thought Lee, are too brave for their own good. But would the men fight like they do without such leadership? It was a terrible thing to try and balance.

Stuart saw the repulse was complete, then rode off himself to arrange troops for his ride to Washington. It was the kind of thing Stuart had been born for: a cavalry raid into the enemy capital. He was tired, but refused to show it. If all it took was the iron will of J. E. B. Stuart to keep himself in the saddle and lead his troops into an action that might win the war for the South, that was an easy thing.

"General Lee," said Longstreet, "Do you wish me to prepare for a counter-attack?" He was hoping Lee would say no, in fact, almost sure that he would, but military protocol dictated that Longstreet should at least offer. An attack after a repulse was normally called for.

"No, General. It is almost dark. We will wait until morning, then repulse another attack which I am sure those people will be compelled to make." Lee peered through his field glasses into the growing darkness, then replaced them to their case which he habitually wore slung across his body. "I wish I knew what the situation was in Vicksburg."

Longstreet did not know either. It was hard to say. If Pemberton had received word that Lee had flanked the Union Army, it would give him more reason to hold out longer. The last anyone had heard, rations were low; men were nearing the breaking point. But news such as this would be like issuing week's rations to the men. Still, hunger will provoke an entire army into rash acts. If they could only get Johnston to help.

Lee was gone again. The poor man, thought Longstreet. His health was not what it had been at the beginning of the war, and this campaign has taken even more out of him. How can a man be expected to spend twenty hours a day in the saddle, and command an army on a campaign, when afflicted with diarrhea? It would almost seem a joke, if it wasn't a killer. Longstreet's troops died more from diarrhea and dysentery at the beginning of the war than from Yankee bullets. Maybe a hundred years from now some historian addicted to trivia will pick up this fact and make something of it. Longstreet chuckled to himself.

* * *

Independence Day
July 4, 1863

"Choose your ground, and make the enemy attack you."

—Napoleon

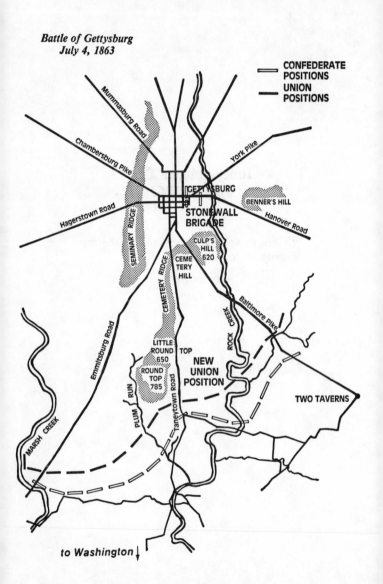

Battle of Gettysburg
July 4, 1863

CONFEDERATE POSITIONS
UNION POSITIONS

Mummasburg Road
Chambersburg Pike
York Pike
Hagerstown Road
Hanover Road
GETTYSBURG
STONEWALL BRIGADE
BENNER'S HILL
SEMINARY RIDGE
CULP'S HILL 620
CEMETERY HILL
CEMETERY RIDGE
Emmitsburg Road
Baltimore Pike
ROCK CREEK
LITTLE ROUND TOP 650
ROUND TOP 785
NEW UNION POSITION
Taneytown Road
PLUM RUN
MARSH CREEK
TWO TAVERNS

to Washington ↓

The troopers adjusted themselves in squeaking saddles. Sabers tucked under girth straps. Captured Yankee carbines in their sockets, then strapped to the trooper himself; in case he was knocked from the saddle, the weapon would go with him. Pistols shined with wood ashes and greased with axle grease from the horse artillery. The order was given, and the long column began its movement. Those eight hours of sleep was like floating to heaven to Stuart's troopers. A little food in their bellies and they were ready to go. After all, they were headed toward the capital of Yankeedom, weren't they?

They ran into Northern skirmishers at dawn outside of Frederick. It upset Stuart that he let the Yankee General French get away, though he did capture some of his staff, and learned from them that French had been ordered to fall back to Washington to protect the capital. How many troops does General French have? They would not tell him that. All right, it's back to General Lee with you, then on to Libby. You may change your minds about talking between here and there.

Stuart immediately closed all the taverns in Frederick. He commanded good men, but the Demon Liquor had ruined more than one military campaign, and this was not one to get stalled because some of the men couldn't stay in the saddles. Stuart himself had never had that problem, and would never as far as he was concerned. They stayed in Frederick only long enought to gather some supplies and a few horses, and information. French had headed back to Washington. They must not have very many troops there. Good information to have.

* * *

They were tired, there was no doubt about that. Marching through the night takes its toll. But they were headed toward Washington, and that buoyed them up immeasurably. They were in Rockville now, where they had captured the wagon train. Here and there along the way, they ran into Yankees; not anything organized, just outposts. The real test would come when they tried to move into Washington. It would be a swift movement—artillery fire against the forts, then a rush. The key to their success is in how many troops Meade had left behind.

Before them suddenly was cavalry. Stretched across the road to Washington, it looked like a regiment. Stuart smiled. Provided they weren't backed up by anything substantial—artillery or infantry—this was a good sign. The Yankees were sending out units to meet the Confederate advance—if they thought they could stop the advance, this would have been several brigades. If it is only a regiment, then that is probably all they have in reserve.

Stuart sends in feelers—two regiments, mounted. The Yankees begin to retire. After they fall back a quarter of a mile, Stuart knows: this is it, this is all they have, and throws a whole brigade into them. The battle is brief. The Confederate horsemen brush aside the Yankees and continue their advance toward the capital of the North.

Two miles south of Rockville, Stuart's men rested for a few hours.

* * *

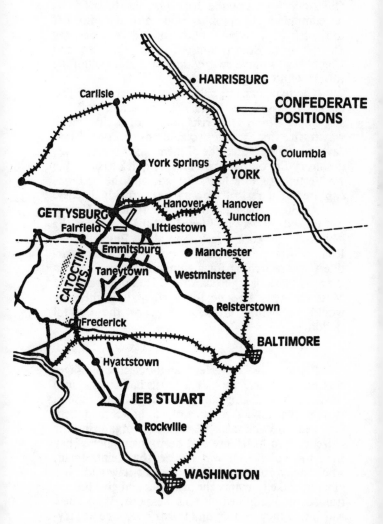

Cavalry Movements
July 4, 1863

HARRISBURG

Carlisle

CONFEDERATE
POSITIONS

Columbia

York Springs

YORK

Hanover
Junction

GETTYSBURG
Fairfield

Hanover

Littlestown

Emmitsburg
Taneytown

Manchester

Westminster

Reisterstown

Frederick

BALTIMORE

Hyattstown

JEB STUART

Rockville

WASHINGTON

One-half mile south of a local imbibery called Old Stone Tavern on the Rockville Pike, Stuart splits his command: Hampton to follow a road leading off to the left, then to bear south again, driving past the District line; Stuart himself, with Fitz Lee and Chambliss to move swiftly down the Rockville Pike toward Old Georgetown.

The two roads paralleled each other as the two columns passed Ft. Reno. The untested, and unsuspecting Union artillerists could not decide which way to fire first, seeing two columns of Confederate cavalry passing either side of them, and the result was desultory fire on both columns. A quick rush by the 1st Virginia of Fitz Lee's Brigade and the fort was captured. The rest of the way was surprisingly easy.

As Stuart headed toward Georgetown, Hampton moved by way of Pierce's Mill Road, past the Mill itself on Rock Creek, and along Piney Branch Road to Massachussetts Avenue. While Stuart's artillery was searching for a commanding position on the hills overlooking Rock Creek, Hampton searched Massachussetts Avenue for a slight hill where he would be within artillery range of the Capitol Building.

* * *

Rumor travelled faster than the electric messages on Chandler's telegraph. The rebels had crossed into the District. Pillaging along the way. Killing, raping, looting, lynching. Two years of war had turned them into vengeful animals. All efforts at organizing the citizenry into a defense had been abandoned. They were too volatile. It was realized by Heintzelman, who finally convinced Halleck, that it would be a great mistake to empty the armories and give the untrained, undisciplined citizens weapons. Who knew which way they would point them? Everyone was trying to get out of town and the bridges were permanently clogged. A wagon in the middle of Long Bridge had caught fire, but fortunately had been extinguished. The wooden bridge would have gone up like matchsticks. The saloons were overflowing with men either wanting one last drink before leaving, or those who were drowning their fears and could not leave. The prostitutes had closed up shop earlier, and taken their highly mobile inventory toward the south. Mercenaries to the end, they were thinking there soon would be much money to be made even if it was in Confederate currency.

* * *

The men were in a jovial, almost giddy mood. Why not, thought Stuart. Resistance so far has been light. The Defenses of Washington were breached with almost no effort whatsoever. It would be difficult to blame anyone for stripping them though. It is much better strategically to fight a battle in front of a capital than to rely only on the immobile forts and heavy artillery. The problem occurs when the enemy out-maneuvers the main army, which is exactly what we did.

The other thought that crossed Stuart's mind was, how organized are the citizens of Washington? Word had leaked out of the frantic preparations that were being suggested, even before the Battles of Gettysburg (which is what, Stuart reckoned, the last few day's affairs would eventually be called) to arm the populace of the city for defense. The lack of troop strength in the forts outside the city was evidence that they had not organized enough yet to send the citizen-soldiers to the outskirts. Stuart dismissed his worries. Never would civilians be able to stand before his seasoned veterans. He had seen his men and horses stand under withering fire, time and again, seated calmly, discussing planting or the weather or common aunts and uncles until one or the other of the speakers was hit, then, after a cursory inquiry as to how bad a wound it was, continue the conversation with another trooper as the wounded man went to the rear. No civilian-trooper, organized within a few days could ever stand against charging horse and screaming rebel cavalryman.

In the distance, Stuart could see smoke over the city. Had Hampton reached the Capitol already? Stuart calculated distances in his head. Impossible. What the devil is going on in the city?

The panic in Washington is like a whirlwind. When the first mounted troopers came galloping back from their defeat at Rockville in the dusk down Pennsylvania Avenue, they didn't have to say a word. Everyone in the town knew, with the swift return of the cavalrymen who were sent out to stop any Confederate advance upon the capital, that the game was up. Stuart, in the growing darkness, could appear in front of Willard's Hotel any second now. And so, as the Union troopers rode past, Willard's emptied, pouring the drunks and the prostitutes out into the street, running every which way, like leaves cartwheeling before the whirlwind.

Omnibuses were stolen, men knocked off their horses and replaced by the thief, who, undoubtedly was knocked from the same horse a block further. Soldiers (what few there were) could hardly move through the congested streets. The mob ruled.

The problem was that there was nowhere to run. J. E. B. Stuart was coming in from the north; to run south would be jumping from the skillet into the embers. But, nevertheless, the Long Bridge was jammed. Stuart was moving in from Rockville. God only knows when he'll come riding down Pennsylvania

Avenue, firing his pistols, red-lined cape and the ostrich-plume from his hat dancing in the wind. Oh, yes, they'd heard about him in Washington. He'll shell the White House, then the Capitol Building, and set the whole town ablaze. Someone in the crowd shouted that they wanted the baboon who'd gotten them into all this. Someone else produced a piece of rope, and a shouting horde of angry, drunken draft-dodgers and southern sympathizers headed toward the White House.

* * *

Lincoln was not there. He was in the Telegraph Office at the War Department with Halleck and Stanton. Outside they heard the commotion of the mobs. The noise hummed below the clicking of the keys. By now the news had worsened. Every time the key chirped it brought more bad news. Meade had changed front to attack the Confederates. His engineers had found virtually no practicable fields of attack against the Confederates who were entrenched along the face of a gentle, open slope toward the Union Army, squarely across the roads leading south. Confederate rifle-pits lined nearly barren slopes, cleared, in many cases, by the Confederates working feverishly through the night—impossible to assault frontally without great losses. The rebel left flank was secured on a ridge on the other side of Marsh Creek and their artillery commanded the bridge. The stream there was fordable, but the water was waist high (and rising because of the recent rain), and the men would be exposed to fire for nearly 800 yards before striking the Confederate rifle-pits. The rebel's right flank was equally as strong with small streams breaking the ground where assaulting troops would cross. Artillery swept the approaches to that flank as well. Cavalry is feeling for a way out, but has run into enemy cavalry particularly to the east. Jenkins and Robertson were doing their jobs.

Stanton said something to Halleck about stripping the defenses of Washington; Halleck brought up the subject of that "idiotic" message that Stanton had sent him about placing batteries along the approaches to the city, and the two started arguing all over again. Lincoln rose and walked to the telegrapher. He wrote out a message on a piece of paper to General U. S. Grant at Vicksburg, Mississippi:

War Department
Washington, D.C. July 4, 1863

General:
It is advised that you should pull back from your present positions of siege. Remain, however, close enough to resume such operations should the situation in and about the Capital allow them. Do not attack or otherwise antagonize the enemy in your front for the time being.
A. Lincoln

Stanton and Halleck stopped arguing long enough to read what the President had written. Halleck was the first to speak.

"You can't mean to call off Grant when Vicksburg is so close to falling, do you?"

"What good would the fall of Vicksburg do us if Washington falls?" said Lincoln. "It appears to me, gentlemen, that we are riding on the back of a lion. The question is, how do we now get off without being eaten?"

* * *

If the South Won Gettysburg

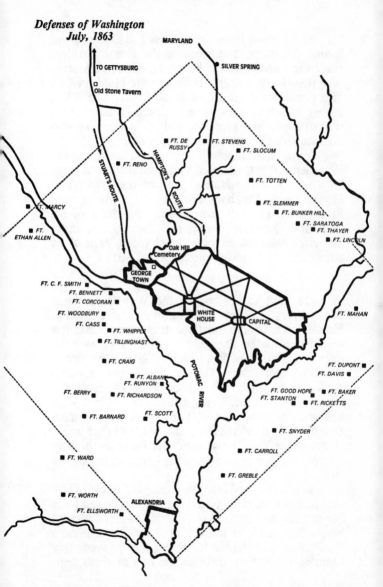

Defenses of Washington
July, 1863

MARYLAND

TO GETTYSBURG
□ Old Stone Tavern

SILVER SPRING

FT. DE RUSSY
FT. STEVENS
FT. SLOCUM

FT. RENO

FT. TOTTEN

FT. SLEMMER
FT. BUNKER HILL
FT. SARATOGA
FT. THAYER
FT. LINCOLN

FT. MARCY

FT. ETHAN ALLEN

STUART'S ROUTE

HAMPTON'S ROUTE

Oak Hill Cemetery

GEORGE TOWN

FT. C. F. SMITH
FT. BENNETT
FT. CORCORAN
FT. WOODBURY
FT. CASS
FT. WHIPPLE
FT. TILLINGHAST

WHITE HOUSE
CAPITAL

FT. MAHAN

FT. CRAIG

FT. ALBANY
FT. RUNYON
FT. BERRY
FT. RICHARDSON
FT. BARNARD
FT. SCOTT

POTOMAC RIVER

FT. DUPONT
FT. DAVIS

FT. GOOD HOPE
FT. STANTON
FT. BAKER
FT. RICKETTS

FT. SNYDER

FT. WARD

FT. CARROLL

FT. GREBLE

FT. WORTH
FT. ELLSWORTH

ALEXANDRIA

At six p.m., Stuart's men reached Georgetown. Major Beckham, commanding the Horse Artillery since the death of their beloved Pelham in March, sent Breathed's Battery to occupy the bluffs in Oak Hill Cemetery overlooking Rock Creek. The White House and War Department looked to be about a mile or a mile and a quarter away. The three-inch ordinance rifles would reach them easily.

Stuart told them to throw several shells into the War Department, then drop just a couple in the front yard of the White House. Do not shell the White House itself. Abraham Lincoln had a young son, Stuart said. Perhaps remembering the death of his own little Flora last November, he would not, under any circumstances, involve the children, even of an enemy, in this blood-gorged viper of war.

* * *

The first explosions in the War Department broke every window in Stanton's office. Lincoln himself ran to the portico, forgetting, Chandler would recall later, the plaid shawl hanging over the door to Stanton's office, which he habitually wore to the Telegraph Room. Out on the portico, Lincoln could see the shells flying through the air, especially when they tumbled. Every one looked as if it were heading right toward him, but he stood erect, unaffected, while they crashed and exploded in the upper floors of the War Department. He becomes the only United States President to ever come under enemy fire.

A shell dropped into the front yard of the White House and exploded. With that Lincoln bolted from the portico and headed toward his home. Later he would be asked if he had not thought of the danger to the President of the United States that he seemingly flaunted by rushing through the hail of shells peppering the White House lawn. He simply replied that for the moment, he had ceased to be the President and became a husband and father concerned only for the welfare of his family and his home. As Lincoln jogged across the White House lawn amid the explosions, Stanton and Halleck appeared, awestruck, on the portico.

As Lincoln disappeared inside the White House, Stanton turned to Halleck. "I think you'd better prepare a carriage and escort for the President to leave the city." Halleck, without a word, turned back into the War Department building. The shelling had stopped for the time being, and Stanton wondered how quickly it would end now that they were making peace so alluring.

* * *

From their positions near the junction of Massachussets and New Jersey Avenues—"English Hill" to the locals because the British had camped there during the War of 1812—Hampton's artillery poured fire into the unfinished Capitol Building with a vengence. It seemed ironic that the largest slaveholder in the South, Wade Hampton, was given the task of shelling the ediface which had echoed for three decades with arguments bent upon destroying the institution that had given him so much. As the shells whistled and exploded in the halls and flew about the scaffolding of the unfinished dome, Hampton thought about his nearly 3,000 slaves and just what he was going to do with them once this war was over. They were valuable, but only in the South. Some of his best darkies were worth $1,000 to $1,500. But who in the South after this expensive war, would be able to buy them from him even if he wanted to sell? Setting them free, in the long run, would be the thing to do. But they are so helpless.

Most of them not being able to take care of themselves, always having been fed and clothed. They were worthless on the international market, even politically detrimental, since Great Britain would not acquiesce to slavery in their trade pacts.

It was a quandry. Everything pointed to freeing them. It was difficult though, to see an institution die. It would almost be like seeing the institution of marriage die out. It was so much within a Southerner, morally as well as socially.

"Could you order your battery to fire a little more to the left, Sir?" said Hampton to one of his battery commanders. Obviously, Congress had fled. It seemed such a shame to destroy such a beautiful building. But this war must end somehow.

* * *

Mobs roamed at will through the streets of the capital that night. The White House was on fire, not from Stuart's shells, but from the angry crowd that braved French's artillery and stormed their barricades. Lincoln and his family had split up—a tearful good-bye, considering that Mary Lincoln believed in her heart that she would never see her husband again. She was nearly hysterical, but he would not allow her to accompany him. The railroad to Baltimore was still open. "You take the first train, Mary. I will follow shortly."

He wanted to be behind in case the train in front was stopped for any reason. Then he would surrender himself to the mob in exchange for his family's release.

(Later, he would be accused of cowardice—that the only reason he had taken the second train was so that if the track was torn up and there was a wreck, he would be able to escape. That thought did not cross his mind, since he knew that both Stuart and

Lee were too well occupied to worry about tearing up some railroad track.)

In Baltimore, as a family once again, they boarded a packet steamer and headed north.

New York was out of the question as a destination for the deposed First Family. There were riots there as well, ostensibly over the draft, but in reality, over the Blacks and Irish immigrants in the city. Both were hung indiscriminantly, the bodies burned and the charred remains dragged through the streets and desecrated. Stores were looted and set afire. The government was in chaos.

Boston seemed stable. Whether Lincoln would be welcomed there, he did not know. He had been criticized recently for his lenient policies toward the South by the Abolitionists in New England, but even when he had issued the Emancipation Proclamation they were not satisfied. They said it freed not a single slave, and they were right since it declared free only the slaves in states in rebellion. But now, it would appear that it was time for all of them to hang together. And, if Boston would not take him, there was always Canada....

* * *

July 5, 1863

Battle of Gettysburg -
Union Assaults
July 4 & 5, 1863

CONFEDERATE POSITIONS
UNION POSITIONS

Mummasburg Road

Chambersburg Pike

York Pike

GETTYSBURG

BENNER'S HILL

Hagerstown Road

Hanover Road

STONEWALL BRIGADE

SEMINARY RIDGE

CULP'S HILL 620

CEMETERY HILL

CEMETERY RIDGE

Baltimore Pike

Emmitsburg Road

LITTLE ROUND TOP 650

ROUND TOP 785

NEW UNION POSITION

ROCK CREEK

July 4 Assaults

TWO TAVERNS

PLUM RUN

Taneytown Road

July 5 Assaults

MARSH CREEK

July 4 Assaults

to Washington ↓

Union assaults were continued on the 5th of July. There was nothing to do but to try and fight their way out. Washington was in a panic. The White House smoldering, Congress abandoned, Lincoln fleeing, and the largest army in the Confederacy between the capital and the army that could save it. Meade took his fearful losses as his cavalry tried to find a flank that could be pried loose. But they were well protected by the terrain and massed artillery.

As the assaults continued through the day, his men were remembering Fredericksburg—how Burnside had thrown them, just seven months ago, time after time, against entrenched Confederates—and were pinning bits of paper with their names and hometowns scrawled upon them to the insides of their blouses, so it would be known where to send the body. Finally, mercifully, darkness came.

Nearly 12,000 losses in the last two days. Staggering. But they might be relieved if French's troops attack Lee's rear. Perhaps tomorrow....

* * *

Meade watched broken-heartedly as the final assault was driven back. His engineers thought they had found a weak spot in the Confederate line near the little town of Barlow on the road to Taneytown. Indeed, the Confederates were in a relatively low area there, and the stream called Rock Creek split their line at that point, but their artillery support on the small ridge behind them had made the difference—artillery at that range for any length of time is devastating on an attacking column. Besides, Meade just didn't have enough troops to send in. After the assaults of the last three days, he just could not kill any more boys. It is over, he thought. I cannot ask them to do any more.

He held a council of war the morning of the 7th

of July. His Corps Commanders (those that were not killed or wounded) voted unanimously to send a request for terms of surrender under a flag of truce. There was no more to be done. Ammunition was dangerously low. If the Confederates decided to attack, they would have no problem over-running the demoralized men under Meade's command. Sedgewick was dead. Hancock wounded very seriously. Two of the finest of his Corps Commanders. The affairs in Washington were so wild and confused, they could expect no help from the government. It was as if the army was the only part of the country still fighting the war. And that could not go on forever. The only thing left to do was to see General Lee, and, as Meade put it to his subordinates, he would rather die a thousand deaths than do that.

* * *

"How many troops do you have left, General Meade?"

Meade sighed heavily. The face of the Commanding General of the Confederate Army seemed too kind. They were enemies, weren't they? And Lee was the victor. He should be flushed with the kill. But instead, he merely seemed very weary. "About 47,000. Possibly less because of desertions." Probably much less, thought Meade, the way the men had been streaming to Harrisburg and Philadelphia.

"All the animals in your army are owned by the government of the United States, is that right?"

"Yes, General."

"It is different in our army. Cavalry and artillerymen have supplied their own horses and mules. Since the animals with your army are government property, I shall have to treat them as captured spoils of war. Except, I think, for the mounts of the officers. Let us allow the officers to keep their horses, and their side arms."

"That will be very well received, General."

"All arms will be stacked beginning at 10:00 a.m. on the 8th of July. Paroles will be supplied, hopefully by then. We are having a little difficulty finding enough paroles for your army. Some of my staff have located a printing press nearby, and are working at producing the number needed. The men will be paroled to go to their homes in the North as soon as possible."

"Some of my men are from Maryland, General Lee. May they go through your lines?"

"Yes, that can be arranged, as long as they pass through at one point. Perhaps along the Baltimore Road. General Longstreet, what do you think?"

"I think my men will be able to pass the small number of Marylanders through. We will work it out." As Longstreet spoke, Meade thought, now, there is the flush of victory—more so in the second in command than in the commander.

"Here is the copy, Sir." Walter Taylor, Lee's adjutant-general handed a copy of the surrender terms to Lee. Lee's eyes scanned the paper carefully. It was only one sheet. One sheet of paper to end the life of this blood-swollen war, and create a new nation. He handed it to General Meade. Meade read it and set it on the table. "I think that will be satisfactory."

* * *

Lord Palmerston, the British Prime Minister, read the article in the Times over twice. Inwardly he was excited—the South in a position to win the war. That should make our people happy. All but the working class, and who can understand why they think the way they do. Parliament will rejoice, Gladstone and Russell will celebrate, but that devil

Milnes, he will be in a tizzy!

Now, thought Palmerston, how do we approach France, then Russia as a united front, to further efforts toward the recognition of the Southern Confederacy so that Great Britain will get the lion's share of the credit. That is the key—to approach France first, but the ambassador to Russia must be kept informed at every turn. So, the South is winning. Somehow I knew their little "experiment" in independence wouldn't work out... A place called *Gettysburg?*

* * *

Pemberton was alone in his bombproof in Vicksburg when he received the scrawled message from Johnston. "Davis says to hold out at all costs. Will help all we can here. Lee is about to capture Wash. J. Johnston."

Pemberton couldn't believe it. The signature was authentic. Even if it had been forged, why would the Yankees want to send a message of hope like this. A moment later, another messenger came in with the same message. Johnston would send two with a message like this, in case one would be captured.

The men were on the verge of mutiny from low rations. This message must be sent out to them. He realized that he must get this to the army as quickly as possible. "Orderly!" he called to the youthful courier who had just left his tent. "Orderly, I want you to spread this message through my army. Go! Now!" Camp rumor. Let them savor it that way first, as they love to. He waited a full minute, then called to his adjutant to bring together his officers. Now, we'll do it officially, he thought.

* * *

They found Wesley Culp's body face down in the rifle-pit he had worked so hard to construct. A bullet through the head, probably in one of the last Yankee attacks on the 5th of July. Some friends buried him under a crooked oak so that his family in Gettysburg could find him later. But they never did.

Shortly after the truce was in effect, an officer from Wesley Culp's regiment called on his sister Julia. She had suspected something had happened when Wes didn't return the night he promised he would. At the sight of the stranger in Confederate gray at her door, she began to cry softly.

"Julia, Wesley is dead," he said after introducing himself. "I'm sorry." He then gave details as to how to reach her brother's grave, then pulled a small package from his pocket.

"I found this on your brother's body. It was wrapped in a note that said if anything happened to him, he wanted these things to be passed on, to stay in the family. The note said he had carried these throughout the war, and wanted them to go to someone who would appreciate them since he had no children."

Julia unwrapped the package. Inside were three pocket knives—two very small and obviously hand-made—and four very old fifty cent pieces. She remembered them as some things a favorite teacher had given Wes, telling him that her grandfather had carried them in another war, and that he should make up a story about them sometime. He never did make up the story, but instead carried them off to his own war.

The Culp family said they never recovered the body, although the burial site was described to them in detail by Wesley's officer when he talked to Julia. Legend began to build upon this unusual claim, and in post-war Gettysburg stories circulated that the family did find his body, and buried the young man who was considered by some of the more outspoken Gettysburgians to be a "traitor", in an unmarked family grave in the Culp plot in the Evergreen Cemetery. Or, some say, he was buried under the packed earth floor of the cellar of the Culp house near Culp's Hill, around which Wes played as a child, fought as a man, and died as soldier.

* * *

V. The Consequences

"The destiny of States depend upon a moment...."
—Napoleon

"Mr. Stanton, with an attitude like that, these people will never oblige us. Think of Mr. Lincoln. What would his attitude have been?"

Stanton was having no part of it. Vice-president Hamlin may as well have been talking to a brick wall. He was attempting to act as a buffer between Stanton's radical views and the offers that Davis and Stephens were presenting. "All they want is independence, Mr. Stanton. Independence and trade established between the North and the South. It is as simple as that." He mopped his brow.

Fredericksburg, chosen as the site for the Peace Negotiations because it was halfway between Washington and Richmond, was like a bake oven during the week of the talks, and the oppressive heat made tempers short.

The fact that Fredericksburg had been a major Confederate victory in December of 1862 also played upon Stanton's mind.

"Well, I will have no part of it. You, Mr. Hamlin, may sell the future of these United States for a pittance, but I will not. Posterity, Mr. Hamlin. What will posterity say?"

"Mr. Stanton, they have whipped us. The war is over, or at least will be as soon as we can get out of this heat with our signatures upon that paper."

"But they control all the raw materials, or nearly all. We would have to submit to tariffs from our own country or import from Europe. The rebels can name their own price. I don't like it".

"And we have the means of production," Hamlin said. "How can they gather the raw materials efficiently without our machines? And what good would it do them? Without our factories, they are lost. Now that the war is coming to an end, we will have the manpower to build more factories, and money to pour into them. And, we have not been de-

vastated by the war as the South has. It will be another year, maybe two, before they can supply
enough raw materials for the factories we have. I say,
if they want their independence, let them have it and
be damned. They will come back to us, on our terms,
soon enough.''

Stanton mulled this over in his mind. What he
really wanted was revenge, to punish these uppity
Southerners for all the trouble they have caused. This
was the one huge bone of contention between Lincoln and himself—Lincoln wanted to ease them back
into the Union, as if they had never separated. But
Lincoln was wrong. These were people in rebellion
against their government—traitors, and should be
punished like traitors. And here we are discussing
peace with them. We should be watching them climb
the scaffold. It made Stanton almost sick to his
stomach. If Halleck and Lincoln had only listened to
him.

"Mr. Stanton, we have to go back into that
room and speak with Mr. Stephens soon. It has been
two weeks since Meade surrendered. Mr. Lincoln is
gone, the capital is gone, the Congress....Please Mr.
Stanton.''

"You, sir, may put your name on that document
with the rest of the traitors, but I will never. What
will the future say of us?''

The Document of Peace between the United
States and the Confederate States of America was
signed without Stanton. In addition to re-establishing
trade between the two countries, the North agreed to
pull U.S. troops out of the South and dissolve the
blockade of Southern ports. One month after all
U.S. troops withdraw from Southern states, Confederate troops will end their occupation of Washington
D.C. and the United States government will establish
itself again in the Northern Capital.

Some of the more radical people in the North thought that the government had given up too soon—that, given six more months, the blockade would have tightened up even more, leaving the South to the ravages of attrition. They particularly pointed to the fact that Vicksburg was about to fall, which would have split the South in two.

But more realistic people in the North knew that without the stabilizing influence in Washington, the various splinter groups in the North could never have pulled together strongly enough to defeat the Confederacy. The Radical Republicans wanted revenge. The Abolitionists wanted freedom for the slaves at any cost. The Peace Democrats, led by Clement Vallandingham, were singing in the streets while Stanton had sulked in Fredericksburg. Politically, the situation in the North was similar to how it was before the 1860 elections, except that in 1860, at least there was an existing President and Congress.

It was decided that as Confederate troops marched out of Washington, Union troops would march in, to establish temporary martial law until Congress re-convened.

The scene was strange indeed: Confederate troops marching victoriously through the streets of Washington D.C. on their way south. They sang, and their bands played "Dixie", but there were no cheers from the "liberated" populace (but no anti-Southern sentiment displayed either), and no scenes of drunken celebration by Confederate soldiers in the streets. The town was deserted. With the exception of Stuart's men, who met the rest of their army, and a few civilian onlookers, Washington was a ghost town. The celebrations will have to wait, thought more than one Confederate soldier as they crossed the Long Bridge into Virginia, until we get to Richmond.

In 1865, the former General Robert E. Lee, the hero of the Battle of Gettysburg and consequently the war, is offered the nomination for President of the Confederate States of America. In a moving speech before thousands of his veterans in Richmond, he respectfully declines the offer, mentioning his physical condition as the main reason for not wanting to pursue the rigors of a political campaign, but intimating that, by training, he was "but a soldier" and, in his opinion, while qualified for leadership on the battlefield, he was not so qualified in politics.

The speech only adds to the already growing aura surrounding Lee. (There was a story circulating concerning the time Lee was travelling and was caught by the darkness and forced to stay at the home of one of his veterans for the night. The old Confederate was asked what it was like to share sleeping accommodations with the reknowned General. "I didn't sleep a wink," he said. "It was like sleeping with God.") Lee is revered by both Southerners and Northerners alike for his unceasing efforts towards the re-establishment of ties between the Confederate States of America and the United States. Not even the Radical Republicans of the North, while having no problems finding enemies in nearly every other personage, could argue against his simple but noble grace. His tactics at Gettysburg become the subject of dozens of books, and while praising his subordinates and Almighty God for the victory, he humbly accepts the acclaim for the battle called "Perfect".

Lee's death in 1870 brought both Northerners and Southerners together in mutual grief. Conspicuous as a pallbearer in the funeral was George Gordon Meade, Lee's old adversary at Gettysburg.

* * *

Westward expansion across the face of America was turning into a footrace between disillusioned Northern war veterans and Southerners who saw post-war prosperity in the land and mineral resources of the West. It was almost like before the war when Slavers and Abolitionists raced to see who could swing the votes one way or the other.

Northerners had somewhat of an edge at first. The completion of the Trans-continental Railroad and branches of the road leading to the big cities of the North gave them a temporary advantage in mobility that the Southerners (behind the times still, in the late 60's and early 70's because of the lack of foundries in the South) did not enjoy. It was not until the great mobilization for the Cuban War that factories and foundries began to grow.

(Many historian like to speculate how the Civil War would have turned out had it lasted another two or three years. The North, having the manufacturing centers for arms and cannon, would seemingly have had the edge. Common sense would say that if the war became one of attrition against the South, the North most certainly would have won. But, dyed in the wool Confederates continued to counter the historians by saying that as long as the North kept making the arms, their troops would have kept capturing them!)

Instead of expanding westward, the South began to expand southward, to Mexico, Central and South America, especially after the Cuban War and the Pact of Expansion with France. This expansion is considered by historians, to be one of the most important moves (next to secession) in Confederate History.

* * *

It is fortunate for the South that the Cuban War broke out when it did. By 1868, the Confederacy had bolstered its military power to early Civil War strengths. Although the old Army of Northern Virginia and the Army of Tennessee (as well as the rest of the major Southern wartime armies) were no longer in existence, the individual companies and regiments, being locally formed, continued to drill weekly (as they had as militia outfits in pre-Civil War days) and, once every three months, had maneuvers. The modern National Guard in the North had its roots in this Southern tradition that was kept up even in times of peace.

So when European Imperialism sought to manifest itself in Cuba and South America, the Confederate States of America was prepared to oppose it.

C. S. A. troops were landed on the island of Cuba. Fighting under many of their old commanders of the Civil War, they won several decisive battles. The Spanish hold on the island was pried loose within the year.

The French in Mexico, seeing this display of military strength by the Southerners, and deciding against waging a costly overseas war, established negotiations with the Confederates. From these negotiations came the Pact of Expansion, limiting French expansion in South America, and allowing Southerners to settle in parts of French South America.

* * *

The political and economic pressure over the issue of slavery being put on the Confederate States of America had reached its peak in the 1870's. Internationally, England had always been against it, although they had backed the Confederate cause clandestinely during the war; France followed England, and Russia wasn't far behind in demanding the release of blacks from bondage, even though the elitists in Russia still believed in their own form of slavery.

But the anti-slavery bloc was headed by the Confederacy's neighbor to the north, the United States. By 1873, the threatened boycott of Southern goods and trade forced the state governments to offer to subsidize the slaveholders in the South for the cost of the slaves still held in bondage.

The Subsidy Plan was met, however, with a great deal of antagonism from many Confederate Congressmen. Many of the slaveholders themselves agreed with non-slave-holders in wondering why state funds should be used to pay for the freeing of slaves—property purchased originally by another generation of Southerners. The arguments for the Subsidy Plan ran something like this: land that has been handed down from generation to generation must be paid for by a purchaser. The arguments against: Slaves were not property like land; the were human beings (a fact the Abolitionists had tried to drive home in pre-war days), and, more importantly, why should tax money be used to buy slaves when many of the taxpayers had already released their slaves years before (at a loss to them) or had never held slaves to begin with.

The Subsidy Plan was replaced by a States Tax Incentive Plan, allowing slaveholders who released their slaves within a two year period tremendous tax advantages for those two years, and tax penalties for those who did not comply in time.

Most of the slaveholders complied immediately with the request to release the slaves. The fact was, it simply did not pay anymore to feed, clothe, house, and care for the medical needs of a large group of slaves (and their dependents). Machines were being developed in the North and purchased in the South with money saved in this tax incentive plan that could do the work of ten field hands in one day.

By the Centennial Year of 1876, virtually all of the slaves in the Western Hemisphere (with the exception of a few Southerners who had moved to South America and taken their slaves with them) were free. Contributions from all over the world came into the newly formed Freedom's Bureau, which used the money to establish schools to educate former slaves and find them employment in both the Confederate States of America and the United States.

* * *

The so-called "Balkanization of North America" came sooner than anyone expected. Secession, having been proven to the North on the battlefield to be a right of sovereign states, allowed that any state could now secede from the United States, at the risk, of course, of another Civil War for its independence. In the South, however, the right of secession had been proven by the sword, to be constitutional (a theory which the Southern politicians had adhered to prior to the Civil War). Hence, this allowed any state in the Confederacy to secede from the Confederate States without fear of reprisal from the Confederate government.

By the summer of 1865, Texas was agitating for independence, and the rapidly growing West was considering seceeding from the country. At least, the population of California was discussing it, and the rest of the sparsely populated West was echoing California's arguments.

The area west of the Rockies, primarily because of its geographical isolation, seceeded from the United States almost before the politicians in Washington knew about it. California had never been much of a supporter of the United States even during the Civil War. She had sent money to supply some "California Regiments" (made up of Pennsylvania troops) but sent virtually no men. So, by the 1870's the Republics of Texas, California, and the Rocky Mountains had set up their own separate governments, trade agreements, monetary systems, and diplomacies with the United States, the Confederate States, and the rest of the world.

Many historians speculate about the economic effects of the Balkanization of the continent. Until the United Trade Institution was established in 1883, inflation was spiralling upward, especially in the North. Gold was rapidly being replaced (since it was becoming scarce in Northern coffers) by Greenbacks—paper money with no gold behind it. The Confederacy as well has its problems, having to devalue its Confederate money several times after the war. It seemed that every time the government (be it U. S. or C. S.) stepped in and tried to straighten things out economically, inflation grew worse. And nothing rankled the independence-loving Southerners more than a large federal government meddling with the money and driving prices up. After all, they asked, what did we fight the war over?

California, isolated and with a laissez-faire philosophy concerning their general market, seemed to prosper. The fact that their economy was backed by gold (which was continually being discovered there until the turn of the century) naturally helped California in the international market. Texas would not begin to prosper until the United States began to require more and more oil and petroleum products for its factories, homes, and transportation in the first two decades of the Twentieth Century.

A factor that helped Texas begin its rise to prosperity in the last part of the Nineteenth Century, and, as well, helped bring the Balkanized sections closer together, was not petroleum, nor diplomacy, but an invention.

The development of refrigerated railroad cars and the consequent establishment of railways between large cities of the north and railheads in the west and southwest, brought beef to the very doorsteps of Northerners. Food. Steaks and lamb chops and bacon, brought to Northern housewives from slaughterhouses in the midwest in refrigerated cars stimulated economic growth almost as much as the war did.

Cattle, raised on the grassy plains of Texas, were driven to the railheads and transported, at first, to slaughterhouses in the cities. Later, the slaughterhouses were established near the railheads, and great sides of beef were transported long distances, to the cities. The railroads began to draw the Balkanized sections of the continent together, and cities began to grow near the railheads and slaughterhouses. The sections of the continent were being drawn closer, if not politically, then economically.

There was a rift in economic relations late in the century. The inflated currency in the North could not stand the pressure being put upon it. Between the politicians assuring everyone in the North (and attempting to assure everyone in the rest of the world) that the U. S. dollar was sound, and the reality of the situation in terms of buying power of the dollar, as far as the rest of the continent was concerned, trade between the North and the other republic on the continent slowed to a virtual standstill. The South and West with their incredible amounts of raw materials, turned to foreign markets for their business. Japan, with it's growing flotilla of merchant marine vessels, began to use ports in California more and more frequently. The fluctuation of value between the U. S.

and Confederate currency became as unpredictable as the whims of the politicians. For several years the rest of the world simply bypassed the two countries and dealt with California and the Republic of the Rocky Mountains. By the time the United Trade Institution was established, California was on its way to becoming one of the richest countries in the world.

* * *

In the late 1870's and early 1880's, World Imperialism ran rampant. The Monroe Doctrine was virtually forgotten. Europeans settled in South America in droves, beginning with the French expanding southward from their 1860's strongholds in Mexico.

Japan and China began to dominate Eurasia. Several small wars were fought over Indo-China between the two emerging nations, but the most significant occurrence in the last decade of the Nineteenth Century was the growth of Japan's Navy. Like the island country of England in the 18th and 19th Centuries, Japan began to realize that its future lay in the development of not only a large merchant marine, to keep up its growing trade with California and the Republic of the Rockies, but also in the development of a powerful Navy. Taking many of the lessons learned by the North as it developed a Navy to blockade the South in the Civil War, Japan experimented with ironclads and steam powered warships. Japanese ships were seen from the ports of France to South Africa to San Francisco. Some North Americans expressed a fear that was to be later realized: Japan would someday be a power to be reckoned with.

* * *

Southerners were appalled at the growing problems of discrimination and segregation in the North. The turn of the century brought to the United States what became known as the Jim Crow Laws, named after a traditional song and dance of the South. Southern social analysts blamed the animosities felt in the North against the former slaves on several things.

First, there was the idea that the Civil War had, in essence, been a "Black Man's War" in which hundreds of thousands of Northern boys had sacrificed life and limb for the emancipation of the black man. The woes that beset the nation after the war needed some focal point, and the poor, uneducated former slave—the stranger to Northerners—had to be the scapegoat.

In addition, the freeing of the slaves flooded the job market with workers who were willing to work for "slave wages", much less than the ex-Union soldiers who were also looking for jobs at the end of the war in 1863. Many veterans were fired from jobs and replaced by ex-slaves. The results were isolated riots throughout the North over nearly a decade.

The Southerner's more lenient attitudes stemmed from generations of dealing with the blacks, and to the continuing feeling of belonging to an aristocratic class of people. Even the poorest of the Southerners felt better than the black man who was once servile to the whites, and certainly felt superior to the new "white trash"—the immigrants who were streaming to Northern ports and big cities in droves.

Big Business in the North, with a multitude of cheap laborers, profited incredibly. The white middle-class Northerner, who probably fought the Civil War because he felt in his heart that it was not right to hold men in bondage, was now suffering for his efforts.

* * *

If the South Won Gettysburg

The South watched with sordid interest as President Franklin D. Roosevelt initiated the first United States Federal Income Tax. His expanded governmental programs, begun to help bail out the people hit hardest by the Depression, must have funding from somewhere, and the Federal Income Tax seemed the solution.

The Confederacy never had a country-wide tax. Each state was to supply its own monies from state sales and property taxes, which, of course, had gone higher each year (with a few rare exceptions over the years) to fund statewide programs. The state taxes were, on the whole, much higher than the Federal Income Tax. But Social Security witholdings were (and to this day are) non-existent in the South.

The small town, rural atmosphere pervaded the South. A neighbor-helping-neighbor attitude reflected itself in nearly every phase of business. Perhaps because they knew that no large Federal grants or guaranteed loans were available, the Southern businessman was more conservative in the main, than his Northern counter-part. The Great Depression of the 1930's was not felt quite as severely in the South because fewer merchants and businessmen relied upon financing from big, federally insured banks. In fact, some Southern businessmen actually prospered during the 30's by buying businesses in the North and financing them through local, hometown banks.

* * *

To combat the economic woes of the 1930's the United States government began taking moves that made Southerners very thankful for far-sighted ancestors such as Jefferson Davis and Robert E. Lee. The Federal government was going into business to help the country out of its depression. It was ludicrous to most Southerners—Social Security, Banking, Food, Gasoline—the idea of the Federal government stepping into anything on the general market and controlling (or attempting to control) prices or demand, was contrary to everything they had been taught or believed in about what the founders of America had in mind. If taxpayers' money was being used to finance something that is available on the free market, then, in essence, the taxpayer is paying for something whether he receives that item or not.

There was the famous case of the Independent Telephone Company in Marietta, Georgia. The company employed several hundred of the townspeople, enough to represent a fairly large segment of the working population. When the company was on the verge of bankruptcy, the employees themselves bought up a special edition of stock, issued upon their insistence, just for the crisis. The employees were willing to invest in the company to save their jobs. With the employee's investments and local bank loans, the company began a whole new line of modern telephones, wider services, and progressive advertising. Within months I. T. C. began hiring more people from the town of Marietta.

Had this happened in the North, Southerners were certain that before the employees themselves could work out a solution, the Federal government would have stepped in, and either bought up I. T. C., subsidized it, or loaned it the money to continue employing the people in Marietta. In other words, people in Miami or Richmond would be paying for telephones and service they would never see or use, in faraway Marietta, Georgia. The Southerners were even more convinced in the 1930's of the advantages of the outcome of the Civil War.

* * *

The atmosphere of independence pervaded not only the domestic and intra-continental affairs of the Confederacy, but international affairs as well.

England had remained a close supporter of the South after the war ended, and was drawn even closer after the institution of slavery was abolished. Trade relations were excellent. Technology as well as culture were passed between the two countries, and England always felt closer to the more cultured pre-war South than the North. Perhaps this is why, when affairs in Europe seethed and Germany declared war on England in 1914, many Southerners enlisted in the Royal Canadian Air Force to fight for England even before the Confederacy's formal declaration of war upon the Central Powers of Europe in 1916. When he United States declared war on the Central Powers almost a year later, the North and South found themselves strange bedfellows, allied in war, and closer in ideology than they had been since before the Civil War.

* * *

After the Great World War, the United States moved into a new era in International Relations. The War, of course, stimulated Northern economy, but more than that, gave Northerners a new sense of worth, something they had seemingly lacked since the end of the American Civil War. During the 1920's, life in the United States became a gay and carefree frolic, and Northerners abroad displayed a naiveté that made them stand out in a crowd.

Southerners, on the other hand, seemed to pull back from international affairs and become more introspective. The Great War had ravaged much of Europe and Southerners could empathize with them, remembering the stories their parents and grandparents told of the victorious, but nearly destroyed

South. The Era of Southern Expansionism was being replaced by an era of Conservatism, which later, as the rest of the world spiralled downward into another more horrible world conflict, would become an era of Pacifism.

One of the major pieces of legislation passed by the Confederate Congress as well as all the individual states during the Era of Conservatism, was a bill encouraging a voluntary limit of dependence upon foreign countries for raw materials. Once again, the attitude of independence for which the Civil War was fought (and upon which the entire country, North and South was once founded upon) became the fulcrum upon which all legislative decisions turned.

Northerners scoffed at the "old time" thinking and ideals of self-reliance and hard work displayed in the South. Why now, Northerners asked, when credit was easy and the world was available for enjoyment, were Southerners turning inward. Never, Northerners said, in today's every-shrinking world, could the Confederacy maintain a standard of living as high as the North's without dealing with the rest of the world. Some Confederates agreed with this thinking, but most continued their strivings for independence on their own terms.

* * *

During the late 1930's there was a revival of interest in the Civil War Era of the history of the Continent. People became Civil War "buffs", and the school of thought known in academic circles as "Revisionist" began to bloom. In general, the continent began a soul-searching as to the causes and effects of the American Civil War upon America and the World.

Some people think it may have started with a simple letter-to-the-editor of the Richmond Enquirer which was received on July 1, 1938, exactly 75 years to the day after the beginning of the Battle of Gettysburg. Upon that occasion, said the letter's author, it would be appropriate to re-examine the history of the Confederacy and the United States with reference to the rest of the World and the future, in terms of one simple question: What if the South had lost Gettysburg?

He recalled to the readers the hunger in Richmond, the destruction in Fredericksburg and Vicksburg, the oppression in New Orleans while under enemy occupation, and the intimate agony of the families who saw sons march away, never to return.

And, he asked, what if the South had lost at Gettysburg? What if Lee had been forced to retreat, and the war had lasted another two, three, or four years. Most assuredly, he said, the South would have lost the war to attrition, and the hunger in Richmond, and destruction, and oppression of the first two years of the war would have been merely a mild foreshadowing of what would have come.

If, he said, the United States, or California, or the Rockies wished to understand what was going on in the hearts of people in Europe, and particularly, in Germany, look to the South, and imagine what it would have been like to be a Southerner had the war lasted a few more years. The defeat, the hunger, the loss of family, the oppression of occupation, are things that Germans had grown up with since the Great War. It is easy to understand why now they grope for any leader, even a Hitler, to take them away from their past.

And, he said, it was fortunate the Civil War had not lasted another four or five years after Gettysburg, for the signs of a future under those conditions, as we see from Germany, are ominous indeed.

The letter was signed "R. E. L. Beauchamps. Bogota, Columbia, South America."

The return address is what prompted the editor of the Enquirer to send a reporter to South America to find Mr. Beauchamps, and do a story on such an ardent Confederate living in South America.

The reporter returned with a series of articles that were printed in almost every major newspaper on the Continent. He had found that shortly after the pact limiting French expansion in South America and allowing Confederates to settle there, some Southerners had bought large amounts of land and moved entire families, slaves and all, into South America. They established an Ante-bellum climate wherever they could, working large plantations to grow cotton, tobacco, sugar, and even coffee, using their slaves (which were not effected by the individual Southern States Tax Incentive for releasing them) and the cheap South American labor. The reporter found that Mr. Beauchamps was not the only plantation owner in South America, and that, in fact, there were literally hundreds of resettled Confederates. Large, Georgian style mansions had been built, balls and cotillions were thrown, picnics and barbeques were the coming out parties for the young "Belles" of the new South America. It was almost as if the clock had been turned back to 1850, and time had stood still.

* * *

Appendix

Appendix—Tactics in the Civil War

Tactics, as it is taught at West Point, can be a very complicated affair. But tactics, as it was taught to and used by Civil War officers, relies mostly upon common sense. As the Civil War officer might see it, tactics involves common sense applied to the capabilities of men and weapons, and the advantages of the battlefield terrain.

There were a few simple rules to remember when establishing a position for troops in a Civil War battle. First and foremost, gain the high ground. In doing so you will assure yourself that if the enemy attacks you, he must first climb the hill or ridge you're on to get to you. He will be tired and less effective by the time he strikes your line. In addition, you, being on a hill or ridge, can hide reserve troops behind your position where the enemy cannot see them; he must expose all his attacking force to you in an attack upon your position. When digging in, make your entrenchments down the side of the hill a little way, so that you are not silhouetted along the top of the hill. And, when digging in, be sure to clear a field of fire in front of your position—chop down trees for 60 or so yards so that the attacking enemy must cross an open area where you can see him and fire upon him.

Secondly, have some obstacle over which the enemy must advance. Leave some of the trees you chopped down while clearing a field of fire—enough to break the enemy's formations, but not enough to afford him protection. Find a position with a stream running before it to slow down an attacker. If it is deep enough, enemy troops must raise their weapons and ammunition above their heads to keep them dry. They are unable to fire at you for a while, when you can fire at them. A river before your position is even better. The enemy must utilize fords or bridges to cross—he must concentrate his troops in one small area at the crossing, giving you a cluster of troops to fire at. Rocks or rough ground, or even man-made obstacles over which an enemy must advance all help you to defend a position—they break his ranks and add to confusion on an already smokey, noisy battlefield.

Finally, after having established your battleline on a ridge, with a stream before you and rocky, rough ground for the enemy to advance across, you must secure the end of your line from attack. The "flank" or end of a battleline is always the most vulnerable. Civil War reports are filled with "flank movements" that, when successful, have changed the course of a battle. If the enemy can strike your flank, he has a good chance of getting around behind you as well.

The inherent weakness in the Napoleonic formations used on the battlefield by Civil War tacticians was that they consisted basically of two ranks—a front rank and a rear rank:

Direction of Fire

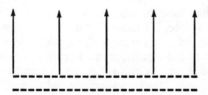

The direction of all the fire-power of this formation is to the front. Where a battleline could bring several hundred weapons to bear towards the front, should they be suddenly attacked on the flank, they could at first, only bring two or maybe three weapons to bear in that direction, while the enemy is bringing their full fire power to bear upon them—several hundred bullets screaming down the length of the line, with men being hit in the side and the back. It was one thing to face an enemy firing at you, a completely different thing for him to be firing from the side or rear when you couldn't fire back.

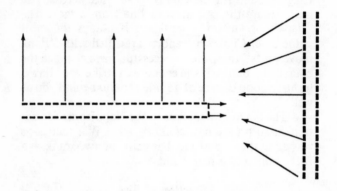

Therefore, it was essential for a Civil War officer, when securing a position, to secure the weakest part of his line, his flank. He must utilize natural or contrived defenses, placing the flank upon a hill, or hiding it in the woods, or anchoring it along a river when the enemy cannot get around behind it readily. Support the flanks especially with artillery or cavalry, and always when possible, entrench.

* * *

Appendix—Tactics vs. Technology

Tactics, from the beginning of warfare, have been dictated by the capabilities of men and weapons, and the utilization of the battlefield's terrain to the best advantage. Napoleon once said that an army can go anywhere a man can place his foot. Strategically speaking, and with leeway for considerations of supply, this is true. However, when we apply this statement to the battlefield, (tactics begin on a smaller scale than grand strategy), we have to modify it to say an army can go anywhere a man can place his foot—provided he is not within the range of the enemy's guns for very long.

In Napoleon's time, around 1800, the massed attack was the thing. Men lined up shoulder-to-shoulder, in waves of ranks, and assaulted a line of the enemy. They could march calmly (enduring artillery fire, of course) to within 100 yards or less of the enemy (the effective range of the smoothbore muskets being 100 yards), fire a volley, then charge on the run, bayonets fixed, for hand-to-hand fighting. In the fifteen or twenty seconds it would take them to sprint across the area within the 100 yard range of the enemy's muskets, they would take only one volley from their opponents—the muzzle-loading muskets could not be loaded any quicker than that—before they were upon them for in-close combat. The day would be won at the point of the bayonet.

In 1849, a Captain Minie of the French Army, invented a bullet that would someday revolutionize infantry tactics. Unfortunately for several hundred thousand American boys who died because the tacticians had not caught on to the effects of weapons technology, that someday would come too late.

Minie's bullet, known to Civil War soldiers as the "Minnie Ball," was neither small, as its first name implies, nor round. It was an elongated conical cylinder, made out of soft lead, .58 caliber (nearly one-half inch in diameter), and weighing almost an ounce. The key to this bullet was in its base, which was hollowed out. This hollow space provided a place for expanding gases, caused by the ignition of the black powder within the barrel of the weapon, to enter. The hot gases softened the lead from the inside of the bullet, and the gases' expanding pushed the walls of the hollowed-out area outward, tight against the inside of the barrel of the weapon.

When the minnie ball was used in a rifled weapon—rifling being a series of twisting grooves within the barrel of the weapon (known since before Napoleon's time, but relatively uneffective until the advent of the minnie ball)—the effect was tremendous. The soft lead filled the grooves tightly so that very little gas escaped and all its force was directed toward pushing the minnie ball on its deadly mission. As it exited, the rifling imparted a spin to the bullet (sort of like a spiral when throwing a football) which caused it to travel more accurately and much farther than the round ball formerly used. Nearly 400 yards farther, as a matter of fact.

What this meant to an attacking column is this: No longer could they advance at a leisurely pace across a field to within 100 yards of the enemy. Now they were drawing fire at 300 to 400 yards, and were easy targets since their commanders were still using Napoleon's tactics and shoulder-to-shoulder formations. No group no men could sprint 300 yards across cornfields, broken terrain, plowed areas, and still be expected to have enough energy left to fight hand-to-hand. So, in the last 300 yards or so of their attack, they were subjected to 5 or 6 volleys from the defenders, while they maintained their energy-saving march-step—and took their appalling losses.

In addition to the problems presented by the new weapons technology, defenders were also getting wiser. Early in the war, at First Manassas, the fighting was done in open fields, using the natural geography—swales, hills, depressions in the land—for cover, or obtaining no cover at all. But as the war progressed, the men and commanders realized that a prepared position—one improved by digging entrenchments and building breastworks in front of the defenders—was the most easily defended with the least amount of losses. Rarely, by 1863, did an army stop for more than an hour with the enemy nearby, without digging in.

Clearly, the day of the grand Napoleonic assault, with banners waving and long lines of bayonets gleaming, was coming to a belated and bloody end. It was becoming the day of the prepared defense. Robert E. Lee was sometimes called, "The King of Spades" for his judicious use of the shovel in the hands of his men whenever they stopped. "Stonewall" Jackson, in his first battle of the Civil War, was informed by a fellow officer that they were being beaten back. "Then Sir," replied Jackson, "we will give them the bayonet!" On his deathbed in May of 1863, he displayed what he had learned about prepared defensive positions and the bayonet-tactics when he said, "My men sometimes fail to drive the

enemy from a position, but they always fail to drive
us away.''

* * *

Appendix—The Confederate Constitution.

The Confederate Constitution was designed around the original United States Constition, and provided basically the same elements: elected officials (but different terms of office, in some cases); two houses of Congress, and so on. In a way, it would seem a little ambiguous to create a constitution for a nation which was supposed to insure non-nationalized freedoms. But some sort of central government was needed, at least in wartime, and so the Confederate Constitution was written.

Some of the improvements included the prohibition of over-sea slave trade; no longer could slaves be brought into the Confederacy from abroad. The United States Constitution made no such provision. The Confederate Constitution prohibited bounties or duties to foster any one particular industry, as well as denying any extra compensation for an individual contractor to the government. After a certain amount of time, the Post Office would be self supporting. The President could not hold the office twice, and his term would last six years.

Slaves were considered rightful property (like cattle, a dog, or a shed) and could be transported into any territory without jeopardizing their status as property. Cabinet members could take part in the debates of the Congress. Subordinate government officials could not be removed by the President without reporting to the Senate his reasons for removal.

All considered, it was an idealistic, but typical revolutionary document. It was a reflection of the Southern Cavalier who was fighting the war, as well as administrating the government. It corrected old injustices to the Southern way of life, and added some new laws to help perpetuate existing injustices to the black man.

Appendix — Organization of the Union Army at Gettysburg

The **Army of the Potomac** (the largest of several Union Armies in the field) is divided into eight (8) **Corps** (average strength—12,125 men):

1st Corps	2nd Corps	3rd Corps	5th Corps	6th Corps	11th Corps	12th Corps	Cavalry Corps

Each Corps is divided into two (2) or three (3) **Divisions** (average strength—4,041):

First Division	Second Division	Third Division

Each Division is divided into two (2) or three (3) **Brigades** (average strength—1,347 men):

First Brigade	Second Brigade	Third Brigade

Each Brigade is divided into several **Regiments** (average strength—336 men):

20th Ind.	3rd Mne.	4th Mne.	86th N.Y.	124th N.Y.	99th Pa.

Each Regiment is divided into several **Companies** (average strength—38-40 men):

Co. A	Co. B	Co. C	Co. D	Co. E	Co. F	Co. G	Co. H

The same attrition from battle and disease that affected the Confederate Army in two years of war took its toll on the Union Army. The average company was reduced by 60-70% by the time the war reached Gettysburg.

Organization of the Confederate Army at Gettysburg

The Army of Northern Virginia (the largest of several Confederate Armies in the field) is divided into three (3) Corps (average strength—25,000):

First Army Corps   Second Army Corps   Third Army Corps

Each Corps is divided into three (3) **Divisions** (average strength—8,333 men):

McLaw's Division   Pickett's Division   Hood's Division

Each Division is divided into four (4) **Brigades** (average strength—1,347 men):

| Kershaw's Brigade | Semmes' Brigade | Barksdale's Brigade | Wofford's Brigade |

Each Brigade is divided into several **Regiments** (average strength—347 men):

| 2nd S.C. | 3rd S.C. | 7th S.C. | 8th S.C. | 15th S.C. | 3rd Battalion |

Each Regiment is divided into several (usually ten) **Companies** (average strength—35-40 men):

| Co. A | Co. B | Co. C | Co. D | Co. E | Co. F | Co. G | Co. H |

As with the Union Army, each Confederate Company was originally intended to contain 100 men. But camp and combat attrition whittled the companies down to 40% of their strength by July of 1863.

Appendix — Union Chain-of-Command at Gettysburg

Major-General George G. Meade
Commanding, Army of the Potomac

Major. Gen. John Reynolds
Commanding, First Corps

Brig. Gen. J. Wadsworth

Brig. Gen. S. Meredith
Brig. Gen. L. Cutler

Brig. Gen. J. Robinson

Brig. Gen. G. Paul
Brig. Gen. H. Baxter

Brig. Gen. T. Rowley

Col. C. Biddle
Col. R. Stone
Brig. Gen. G. Stannard

Col. C. Wainwright (Artillery)

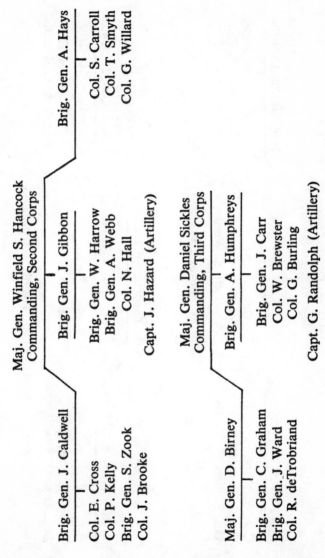

Maj. Gen. Winfield S. Hancock
Commanding, Second Corps

Brig. Gen. A. Hays

Col. S. Carroll
Col. T. Smyth
Col. G. Willard

Brig. Gen. J. Gibbon

Brig. Gen. W. Harrow
Brig. Gen. A. Webb
Col. N. Hall

Capt. J. Hazard (Artillery)

Maj. Gen. Daniel Sickles
Commanding, Third Corps

Brig. Gen. A. Humphreys

Brig. Gen. J. Carr
Col. W. Brewster
Col. G. Burling

Capt. G. Randolph (Artillery)

Brig. Gen. J. Caldwell

Col. E. Cross
Col. P. Kelly
Brig. Gen. S. Zook
Col. J. Brooke

Maj. Gen. D. Birney

Brig. Gen. C. Graham
Brig. Gen. J. Ward
Col. R. deTrobriand

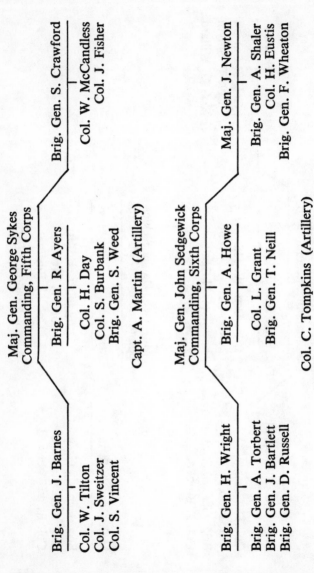

Maj. Gen. George Sykes
Commanding, Fifth Corps

Brig. Gen. J. Barnes

Col. W. Tilton
Col. J. Sweitzer
Col. S. Vincent

Brig. Gen. R. Ayers

Col. H. Day
Col. S. Burbank
Brig. Gen. S. Weed

Capt. A. Martin (Artillery)

Brig. Gen. S. Crawford

Col. W. McCandless
Col. J. Fisher

Maj. Gen. John Sedgewick
Commanding, Sixth Corps

Brig. Gen. H. Wright

Brig. Gen. A. Torbert
Brig. Gen. J. Bartlett
Brig. Gen. D. Russell

Brig. Gen. A. Howe

Col. L. Grant
Brig. Gen. T. Neill

Col. C. Tompkins (Artillery)

Maj. Gen. J. Newton

Brig. Gen. A. Shaler
Col. H. Eustis
Brig. Gen. F. Wheaton

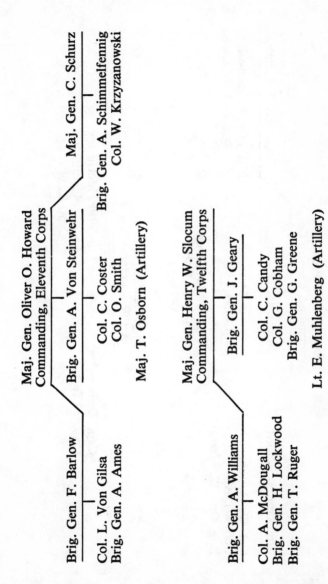

Maj. Gen. Oliver O. Howard
Commanding, Eleventh Corps

Brig. Gen. F. Barlow

Col. L. Von Gilsa
Brig. Gen. A. Ames

Brig. Gen. A. Von Steinwehr

Col. C. Coster
Col. O. Smith

Maj. T. Osborn (Artillery)

Maj. Gen. C. Schurz

Brig. Gen. A. Schimmelfennig
Col. W. Krzyzanowski

Maj. Gen. Henry W. Slocum
Commanding, Twelfth Corps

Brig. Gen. A. Williams

Col. A. McDougall
Brig. Gen. H. Lockwood
Brig. Gen. T. Ruger

Brig. Gen. J. Geary

Col. C. Candy
Col. G. Cobham
Brig. Gen. G. Greene

Lt. E. Muhlenberg (Artillery)

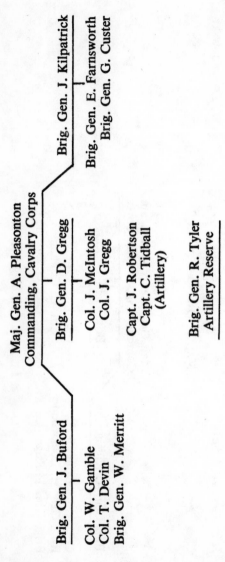

Maj. Gen. A. Pleasonton
Commanding, Cavalry Corps

Brig. Gen. J. Buford

Col. W. Gamble
Col. T. Devin
Brig. Gen. W. Merritt

Brig. Gen. D. Gregg

Col. J. McIntosh
Col. J. Gregg

Capt. J. Robertson
Capt. C. Tidball
(Artillery)

Brig. Gen. J. Kilpatrick

Brig. Gen. E. Farnsworth
Brig. Gen. G. Custer

Brig. Gen. R. Tyler
Artillery Reserve

Capt. D. Ransom
Capt. E. Taft

Lt. Col. F. McGilvery
Capt. J. Huntington
Capt. R. Fitzhugh

Confederate Chain-of-Command at Gettysburg

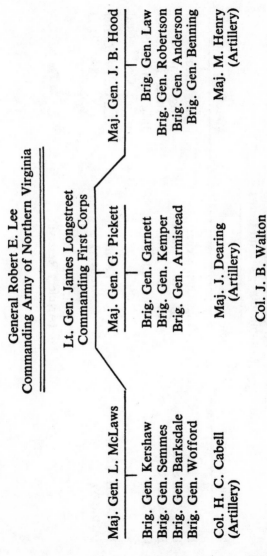

General Robert E. Lee
Commanding Army of Northern Virginia

Lt. Gen. James Longstreet
Commanding First Corps

Maj. Gen. J. B. Hood

Brig. Gen. Law
Brig. Gen. Robertson
Brig. Gen. Anderson
Brig. Gen. Benning

Maj. M. Henry
(Artillery)

Maj. Gen. G. Pickett

Brig. Gen. Garnett
Brig. Gen. Kemper
Brig. Gen. Armistead

Maj. J. Dearing
(Artillery)

Col. J. B. Walton
(Artillery Reserve)

Maj. Gen. L. McLaws

Brig. Gen. Kershaw
Brig. Gen. Semmes
Brig. Gen. Barksdale
Brig. Gen. Wofford

Col. H. C. Cabell
(Artillery)

Lt. Gen. Richard Ewell
Commanding, Second Corps

Maj. Gen. J. Early	Maj. Gen. E. Johnson	Maj. Gen. R. Rodes
Brig. Gen. Hays	Brig. Gen. Steuart	Brig. Gen. Daniel
Brig. Gen. Smith	Brig. Gen. Walker	Brig. Gen. Iverson
Brig. Gen. Gordon	Brig. Gen. Jones	Brig. Gen. Doles
Col. Avery	Col. Williams	Brig. Gen. Ramseur
		Col. O'Neal

Lt. Col. H. Jones
(Artillery)

Maj. Latimer
(Artillery)

Lt. Col. T. Carter
(Artillery)

Col. J. Brown
(Artillery Reserve)

Lt. Gen. A. P. Hill
Commanding, Third Corps

Maj. Gen. R. Anderson	Maj. Gen. H. Heth	Maj. Gen. W. Pender
Brig. Gen. Wilcox	Brig. Gen. Pettigrew	Brig. Gen. Lane
Brig. Gen. Wright	Brig. Gen. Archer	Brig. Gen. Thomas
Brig. Gen. Mahone	Brig. Gen. Davis	Brig. Gen. Scales
Brig. Gen. Posey	Col. Brockenbrough	Col. Perrin
Col. Lang		

Maj. J. Lane (Artillery)	Lt. Col. J. Garnett (Artillery)	Maj. W. Poague (Artillery)
	Col. R. Walker (Artillery Reserve)	

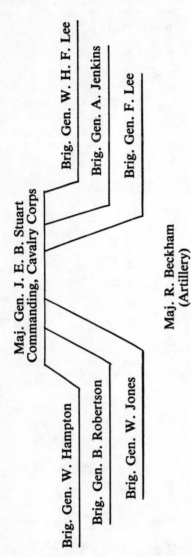

Maj. Gen. J. E. B. Stuart
Commanding, Cavalry Corps

Brig. Gen. W. H. F. Lee

Brig. Gen. A. Jenkins

Brig. Gen. F. Lee

Brig. Gen. W. Hampton

Brig. Gen. B. Robertson

Brig. Gen. W. Jones

Maj. R. Beckham
(Artillery)

Brig. Gen. J. Imboden

Selected Bibliography

Adams, Ephraim Douglass, *Great Britain and the American Civil War*. New York.

Atlas to Accompany the Official Records of the Union and Confederate Armies. Washington, D.C., 1891-1895.

Bachelder Papers, Gettysburg National Military Park Archives, Gettysburg, Pennsylvania.

Bates, David Homer, *Lincoln in the Telegraph Office*. New York, 1939.

Coddington, Edwin B., *The Gettysburg Campaign, A Study in Command*. New York, 1968.

Cooling, Benjamin F., *Symbol, Sword, and Shield*. Hamden, Connecticut, 1975.

Davis, Burke, *Gray Fox*. New York, 1956.

DeRenne, Wymberley Jones, *Lee's Dispatches*. ed. D. S. Freeman, New York, 1915.

Dowdey, Clifford, *Lee*. New York, 1965.

Freeman, Douglass Southall, *Lee's Lieutenants,* Vol. III. New York, 1944.

Grant, U. S., *Personal Memoirs of U. S. Grant,* Vol. I & II. New York, 1885.

Hood, John B. *Advance and Retreat*. ed. Richard N. Current. Bloomington, Ind., 1959.

John Brown's Raid, National Park Service Pamphlet. Washington, D. C., 1973.

Jomini, Antoine Henri, *Summary of the Art of War*. ed. Lt. Col. J. D. Hittle. Washington, D. C., 1947.

Klein, Frederick, *Just South of Gettysburg: Carrol County Maryland in the Civil War*. Westminster, Md., 1963.

Lee, Robert E. Jr., *My Father, General Lee.* New York, 1904.

Long, E. B. with Barbara, *The Civil War Day by Day, An Almanac, 1861-1865.* New York, 1971.

Longstreet, James, *From Manassas to Appomatox, Memoirs of the Civil War in America.* Philadelphia, 1908.

Luvaas, Jay, *The Military Legacy of the Civil War.* Chicago, 1959.

Marshall, Charles, *An Aide-de-Camp of General Lee.* ed. Maj. Gen. Sir Frederick Maurice. Boston, 1927.

Meade, George, *The Life and Letters of George Gordon Meade,* Vol. II. New York, 1913.

Mosby, John S., *Mosby's War Reminiscences, Stuart's Cavalry Campaigns.* New York, 1898.

Plum, William R., *The Military Telegraph during the Civil War in the United States,* Vol. II. Chicago, 1882.

Pollard, Edward A., *The Lost Cause; A New Southern History of the Confederates.* Baltimore, 1867.

Sideman, Belle Becker, and Friedman, Lillian, editors, *Europe Looks at the Civil War.* New York, 1960.

Taylor, Walter H., *Four Years with General Lee,* ed. James I. Robertson. Bloomington, Ind. 1962.

Thomason, John W. Jr., *Jeb Stuart.* New York, 1930.

Tucker, Glenn, *High Tide at Gettysburg, The Campaign in Pennsylvania.* New York, 1958.

Tucker, Glenn, *Lee and Longstreet at Gettysburg.* New York, 1968.

War of the Rebellion: Official Records of the Union and Confederate Armies, Series I., Vol. 27, Parts I, II, and III. Washington, D. C., 1889.

Index

Index

Index

ABOUT THE AUTHOR

Mark Nesbitt was born in Lorain, Ohio, and educated at Baldwin-Wallace College. He read his first book on Gettysburg when he was eight years old, and the study of the battle has been a passion ever since. He worked four years with the National Park Service at Gettysburg as an interpretive ranger giving talks to visitors to the battlefield indoors, outdoors, and even on horseback as a "living history" Civil War cavalryman. He became a freelance writer in 1976.

Although this is his first major work about the battle, he has written scripts for audio stations, slide programs, pamphlets, tours, screenplays, a nationally award winning children's book, and a walking tour of the battlefield for the blind. He lives on six acres in the mountains just a few miles from Gettysburg.

* * *

For additional copies of this book complete order blank and forward with check or money order (no cash or C.O.D.'s) to:

Reliance Publishing Co.
380 Steinwehr Avenue
Gettysburg, PA 17325

Please send _____ copies of ''If the South Won Gettysburg'' at $2.50 each + .50 postage and handling. (PA residents add 6% tax)

Please Print:

Name _____

Street _____

City _____State _____ Zip _____